VEGAN VIETNAMESE DELIGHTS

RAW RECIPES AND BEYOND

Chef Q

Acknowdgement

My name is Quynh, but you might know me as Chef Q. My journey into the world of plant-based eating started in 2014, and it changed my life. Switching to a plant-based diet helped me overcome issues like migraines and depression and taught me the true power of food.

Learning about nutrition opened my eyes to the importance of eating food in its natural state. I embraced a raw vegan diet and discovered the incredible benefits of vitamins, minerals, and enzymes that come from raw foods.

This journey wasn't just about me. I helped others, including my mother-in-law, who added a mostly raw vegan diet to her conventional treatments and saw significant improvements in her health.

Starting this lifestyle doesn't mean making a drastic change overnight. Begin with one meal a day and listen to your body. I believe that Mother Nature has given us the best foods, raw and full of life.

Thank you to everyone who has supported me on this journey. Your encouragement means the world to me, and together, we're moving towards a healthier, happier life with nature's best nourishment.

part 1

INTRODUCTION

Lesson 1

Author introduction

Bui Ngoc Quynh

- Graduated from the Living Light Culinary Institute, the world's first raw-vegan culinary school, specializing in raw-vegan cuisine. Quynh had the privilege of studying under the guidance of Cherie Soria, a pioneer in modern raw-vegan culinary arts.
- Graduated with a Professional Chef de Cuisine degree from Le Cordon Bleu, the world's most prestigious culinary school.
- Holds a certification in plant-based nutrition from Cornell University, ranked among the top 8 universities in the United States.
- Author of two books: '30-Minute Vegan' and 'The Plant-Based Baby Food Cookbook: East Meets West.'

CHEFQ_VEGAN

Lesson 2 — Why raw vegan?

What is raw vegan?

A raw vegan diet is a nutritional regimen that consists of unprocessed plant-based ingredients and avoids cooking temperatures exceeding 46°C. This is to:

- Preserve vitamins and minerals, which degrade at temperatures above 46°C.
- Preserve the natural enzymes found in food.
- Prevent fats from undergoing rancidity.

Benefit of raw vegan

- Promotes health and natural healing.
- Rejuvenates and enhances skin, addressing issues like acne, hyperpigmentation, and aging.
- Improves mental clarity and reduces fatigue and sluggishness.
- Deepens the connection with your body and nature.

Lesson 3 — Equipment preparation

BLENDER

Function

Blend smoothies, plant-based milk, soups, various sauces...

Note

Regular blenders: These blenders are suitable for most basic recipes. However, they might find it challenging to smoothly blend harder ingredients. Continuous use or blending mixtures with low liquid content can lead to overheating, so it's important to use them accordingly to prevent any damage or decrease in performance.

High performance blender: Powerful models like Vitamix, Promix, Blendtec, and others can excel in smooth blending, even with low-liquid mixtures like nut butter. However, they come at a higher cost than standard blenders.

NUT MILK MAKER

Function

Making plant-based milk, porridge, and soups

Note

This tool offers a balance of affordability and efficient performance for smooth blending. However, it may face challenges when working with small quantities or mixtures with minimal liquid, requiring careful adjustment to achieve the desired consistency.

FOOD PROCESSOR

Function

A versatile tool for processing various raw vegan dishes, turning dry nuts into flour, making nut butter, creating thick sauces, cheese...

Can quickly and easily chop, slice, shred, grind, and puree almost tough vegetables like carrots, cauliflower...

Note

Grinding excessively can strain the motor, hindering smooth operation and making it hard to attain a consistent blend. On the other hand, insufficient grinding can lead to food sticking to the sides of the blender, which may also impair the motor. Finding the right balance is key; this is typically determined by the proportion of ingredients to the rotating shaft. To effectively break down food, especially in smaller or tougher quantities, use the 'Pulse' button for better control and results.

JUICER

Function

The benefits of consuming fresh juice are significant as it provides a substantial amount of vitamins, minerals, and beneficial enzymes for the body. These nutrients are preserved to the maximum extent as they are not subjected to heat processing. Additionally, it is the fastest way to deliver and absorb essential nutrients into the body.

Note

Juicing fruits and vegetables is best accomplished with a high-quality cold-press juicer. Compared to centrifugal juicers, slow juicers are more efficient, yielding up to twice the amount of juice and extracting vitamins up to 5-6 times more effectively.

Cold-press juicers excel at processing fibrous and nutrient-rich vegetables like celery, spinach, and curly kale, which centrifugal juicers often struggle with, typically being more suitable for fruit juicing.

When selecting a cold-press juicer, there are two main types to consider: vertical and horizontal. Vertical juicers are generally more compact and easier to clean, while horizontal juicers offer greater versatility, often including attachments for tasks like grinding and mincing.

DEHYDRATOR: ELEVATE RAW FOOD PREPARATION TO A NEW LEVEL

Fuction

Create a variety of cakes using raw vegan ingredients, showcasing the diversity of the diet in dessert preparation.

Dehydrate nuts and fruits to concentrate flavors and create unique textures.

Employ dehydration to remove moisture from foods, which helps prevent the growth of bacteria, yeast, and mold.

Utilize dehydration as a preservation method, helping to maintain the food's nutritional value while extending its shelf life.

Note

If you don't have a dehydrator, consider using alternatives such as an air fryer or an oven set to 45 degrees Celsius.

Remember, costly equipment shouldn't obstruct your journey into raw veganism. Begin with the tools you already possess, experiment with small batches, and only think about investing in more expensive gear once you've mastered the basics.

Lesson 4: Tool preparation

Having the right tools in your kitchen can greatly enhance your raw vegan cooking experience. Here are some essential tools and their specific uses:

KNIFE AND CUTTING BOARD

Crucial for precise chopping and slicing. Detailed instructions provided in Part 4.

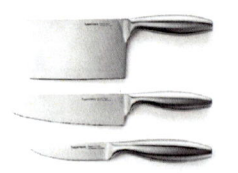

MEASURING CUP OR EQUIVALENT SPOON:

Ensures accuracy in measurements, preventing underfilling or overfilling.

KITCHEN SCALE:
For precise ingredient measurements, especially important in raw cuisine.

SIEVE:
Useful for straining and rinsing ingredients.

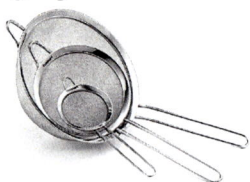

SPATULA: Ideal for mixing and scraping.

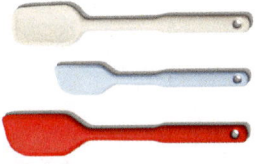

WHISK: Essential for combining ingredients smoothly.

STAINLESS STEEL BOWL: Preferred for mixing due to its durability and ease of cleaning.

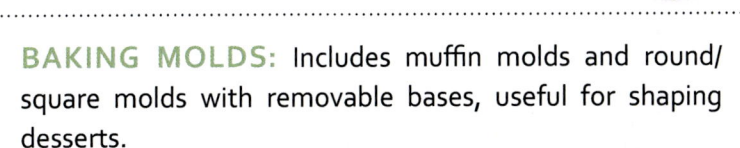

BAKING MOLDS: Includes muffin molds and round/square molds with removable bases, useful for shaping desserts.

ICE CREAM SCOOP: Perfect for portioning and serving dishes like raw vegan ice cream.

Lesson 5 — Food preparation

	STORE OUTSIDE
Fruits and vegetables	• Ripe foods like tomatoes, avocados, and bananas • Dried grapes, cranberries, goji berries
Nuts	• Peanuts • Almonds • Macadamia nuts • Chia seeds • Flaxseeds • Psyllium husk • Ground flaxseeds
Seaweed	• Nori seaweed • Irish moss • Atlantic Dulse

Spices

- Dates, coconut blossom nectar, maple syrup
- Apple cider vinegar, balsamic vinegar, lime juice
- Tamari, Miso, Vegan Fish Sauce, pink salt, sea salt
- Herbs (Fresh, dried, or ground): Cinnamon/cinnamon powder, ginger, scallions, garlic, chili, pepper, mustard…
- Dried European herbs and spices : Thyme, parsley, Basil, Rosemary
- Coconut oil, Peanut oil, Sesame oil, Olive oil

Essential oil

COOL STORAGE

Fruits and vegetables
- Lettuce
- Kale
- Cucumber
- Celery
- Bell Pepper
- Carrot
- Zucchini
- Ginger
- Spring Onion
- Orange, Lemon
- Herbs: coriander, basil, dill

Nuts
- Fresh cashews
- Sunflower seeds
- Pumpkin seeds

Seaweed
- Fresh seaweed : wakame

Spices
- Green pepper
- Vietnamese herbs: Dill, spring onions, chives, mint leaves, basil, perilla, coriander, sawleaf.
- Nutritional Yeast

FREEZER STORAGE

Fruits and vegetables	• Peel ripe bananas/avocados and slice them • Frozen fruits: strawberries, blueberries • Young coconut meat • Frozen coconut water in ice cubes.
Nuts	Fresh Macadamia nuts without dehydration
Seaweeds	Irish moss blended with water, preserved in an ice tray.

Note

Part 2

PRINCIPLE OF COOKING

What makes a delicious dish

1. STRUCTURE: in raw vegan cuisine, the delight of a dish often lies in its texture. A diversity of textures can transform a simple meal into an extraordinary culinary experience. Here's how different textures contribute to a dish: crispy, crunchy, moist, chewy, smooth

Crispy	Elements like nuts and Irish moss add a delightful crispness.
Crunchy	Ingredients such as jicamas, cucumbers, and apples bring a satisfying crunch to meals.
Moist	Citrus fruits and tomatoes introduce a refreshing moisture, balancing drier components.
Chewy	Fresh seaweed, dried apricots, raisins, dried cranberries, and young coconut meat offer a chewy texture that contrasts well with other elements.
Smooth	Avocado, banana, and nut butter create a creamy smoothness that can round out a dish.

Understanding and utilizing these textures can significantly enhance the taste and appeal of raw vegan dishes.

2. FLAVOR: THERE IS A DIVERSITY OF FLAVORS: BITTER, SOUR, SALTY, SWEET, UMAMI.

Sweet:

- A highly pleasing taste for the human palate. From childhood, we tend to favor sweetness in our earliest foods.
- Adds harmony to dishes.
- Some sweet foods: Dates, raisin, sugar, sweet fruits.

Sour:

The Role of Sour Flavors in Raw Vegan Cuisine

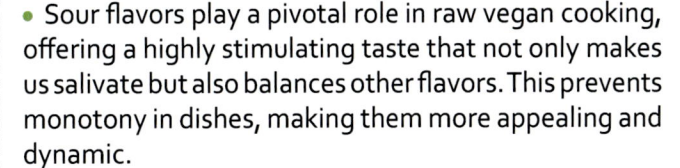

- Sour flavors play a pivotal role in raw vegan cooking, offering a highly stimulating taste that not only makes us salivate but also balances other flavors. This prevents monotony in dishes, making them more appealing and dynamic.
- Softening Vegetables: Sour ingredients like lemons or tamarinds can be used to soften harder vegetables such as carrots, kohlrabi, and jicama, making them more palatable and easier to digest.
- Enhancing Flavors: The tanginess of sour foods can enhance the natural flavors of other ingredients, creating a more complex and satisfying taste profile. Examples of Sour Foods:
- Classic choices include lemons, oranges, and pineapples.
- Tamarinds, with their unique tangy flavor, are also a popular choice in raw vegan dishes.
- Understanding and utilizing sour flavors can significantly elevate the taste experience in raw vegan cuisine, making dishes both delicious and nutritionally balanced.

Salty: 	• Enhances richness and depth of flavor • Salty seasonings: Pink salt, miso, tamari, vegan fish sauce
Bitter:  	• Balances flavors by adding sweet and sour flavors • Use in moderation to avoid overpowering the dish's flavor (as raw food doesn't use high heat to mellow pungent). • Bitter foods: Vegetables, spices, herbs Green leafy vegetables, coriander, basil Pungent taste: onion, garlic, ginger, chili, pepper
Umami:  	Stimulating the Taste Buds in Raw Vegan Cuisine • One of the key aspects of creating an appetizing raw vegan dish is the stimulation of the taste buds, which increases saliva production and enhances the feeling of appetite. • Natural and Ripe Foods: The natural sugars in ripe fruits and vegetables can stimulate the taste buds, making the dish more appealing. • Fermented Foods: Fermentation enhances flavors, adding depth and complexity to raw vegan dishes. • Sun-Drying: While traditional cooking methods like roasting are not used in raw vegan cuisine, similar flavor-enhancing effects can be achieved through sun-drying. This process concentrates the natural sugars in foods, intensifying their flavors. • By incorporating these methods and food choices, raw vegan cuisine can be both flavorful and stimulating, enticing the palate and preparing it for a delightful dining experience. Ripe vegetables(formed from glutamate): onion, ripe tomatoes, kombu seaweed, beets Fermented Foods: miso, tamari sauce, nutritional yeast…

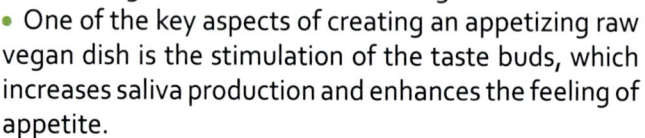

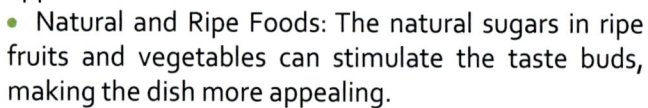

Fat	• Not a flavor but a binding substance that unites all other tastes, prolonging the taste on the taste buds and intensifying richness. • Has the effect of emulsifying and thickening dishes • Natural fat: Avocado, sesame oil, peanut oil, olive oil, cashews, macadamia nuts, coconut flesh, coconut oil...

Lesson 6
Sweet flavor

Dates — One of the finest natural sweeteners in the world, The date's flavor is suitable for dessert recipes such as cakes, nut milk, smoothies, salad dressings...
They can be conveniently used in paste form.

Coconut Blossom Nectar / Coconut Sugar 	Extracted from coconut flowers, it comes in liquid form (commonly known as coconut blossom nectar) or granulated form. This one is rich in nutrients, has a sweet taste and is slightly sour (for nectar). Use: making salad dressings
Maple Syrup 	A superfood rich in nutrients, maple syrup is directly harvested from maple leaf sap and then condensed into syrup form. It has a delightful, mild, and slightly tangy flavor, making it ideal for drizzling on dishes or adding sweetness. However, it can be quite expensive. Uses: baking, salad dressings, soup
Raw sugar 	Some types of sugar undergo a heating process while retaining their nutritional value, such as raw cane sugar, jaggery, monk fruit and jujube syrup.

Lesson 7 — Sour flavor

Apple cider vinegar, balsamic vinegar	The Versatile Role of Vinegar in Raw Vegan Cooking Vinegar is not just a flavor enhancer in raw vegan cuisine; it's also a powerhouse of health benefits. Its inclusion in dishes brings a unique tanginess while contributing positively to digestive health. Enzymes and Gut Health: Vinegar contains enzymes and beneficial gut bacteria that are crucial for a healthy digestive system. These components aid in breaking down food and absorbing nutrients more efficiently. Flavor Enhancement: When used in moderation, vinegar can significantly enhance the flavors of a dish, adding a bright and tangy note that complements the natural taste of raw ingredients. Culinary Applications: It's versatile in culinary uses, from dressings and marinades to adding a zesty touch to raw soups and sauces. Incorporating vinegar into raw vegan recipes not only adds a delightful flavor but also supports overall health, making it a valuable ingredient in this culinary tradition.
Lemon	Known for their zesty sourness, lemons are a powerhouse of vitamins A, E, and B, alongside essential minerals like iron and phosphorus. The color of the lemon, yellow or green, also influences its flavor. Lemons are sweeter with a less bitter peel, whereas limes offer a taste.
Passion fruit	This exotic fruit is not just rich in essential nutrients like vitamins A and C, calcium, potassium, and zinc, but also boasts carotenoids and polyphenols. These powerful antioxidants have the potential to inhibit the growth of cancer cells. Passion fruit's unique aroma also makes it a perfect addition to sauces and dressings, offering a fresh flavor experience.

Kumquat	Rich in vitamin A, C, calcium, potassium, zinc, and other antioxidants. It has a distinctive aroma, adding a unique flavor to sauces and dressings.
Tamarind	With a taste that's a delightful mix of lemon and dates, tamarind is celebrated for its health benefits, including cholesterol reduction and anti-inflammatory properties. It's a versatile ingredient in the kitchen, ideal for dishes like ketchup and salad dressings. Known for its cooling effect, tamarind is also used to create refreshing and hydrating salad dressings, perfect for warmer climates.
Dracontomelon	This Vietnamese fruit can be pickled with sugar to create a refreshing salad dressing.
Apricot	Pickled apricots are not just a culinary delight in raw vegan cuisine; they're also a potent health-supporting food. Their unique properties make them a valuable addition to any raw vegan kitchen. Boosting Immunity and Antioxidant Properties: These apricots are known for their ability to strengthen the immune system and neutralize harmful free radicals in the body, thanks to their rich antioxidant content. Culinary Versatility: sweet pickled apricots can be transformed into an exquisite salad dressing, bringing a delightful balance of sweet and tangy flavors to raw salads. Variety in Taste: It's important to note the taste variations in different apricot varieties. For instance, many imported apricots, like those from Turkey, tend to have a sweeter profile, whereas others may offer a more sour note. Incorporating pickled apricots into your raw vegan diet not only enhances the flavor palette of your dishes but also contributes significantly to your overall health and well-being.

Lesson 8 — Salty flavor

Tamari 	Tamari sauce is a rich and flavorful condiment. It is rich in essential vitamins and minerals, particularly manganese. The fermentation process used in traditional Japanese techniques offers various health benefits. It supports the immune system, heart health, and digestion. Choose tamari sauce made purely from soybeans and naturally fermented for exceptional taste and nutritional value.
Miso paste 	Miso is a versatile and nutritious ingredient. It contains all essential amino acids, making it a complete protein source. Miso aids in digestion and provides a rich source of vitamins and minerals. It supports detoxification, boosts the immune system, and helps reduce bad cholesterol. Miso is commonly used in making vegan cheese, dressings, salad sauces, and more.
Natural Vegan Fish Sauce 	When choosing vegan fish sauce, opt for natural vegan alternatives over industrial condiments. Check the ingredients list to ensure it doesn't contain chemicals or unreadable components. Most natural vegan fish sauces are fermented from ingredients like soybeans and pineapple.

Himalayan pink salt

Pink salt is known for its rich mineral and trace element content compared to regular table salt.
It is often used for pickling vegetables to soften them by breaking down cell structures and releasing water.
These salty flavor enhancers can add depth and complexity to your dishes while also providing various health benefits.

29

Lesson 9 — Bitter flavor

Herbs and Spices	Cinnamon powder, garlic powder, ginger powder, turmeric powder, vanilla pod...	These ingredients act as natural antibiotics for the body, boosting overall health. Additionally, they enrich the flavor of dishes, bringing both nutritional and culinary benefits to your meals.
Vietnamese herbs and spices	Dill, onions, garlic chives, Mint leaves, basil, perilla, coriander, sawleaf,..	These herbs and spices can be used flexibly across a wide range of dishes to enhance their appeal and flavor. Furthermore, in Traditional Vietnamese Medicine, it's believed that the essential oils present in these ingredients play a significant role in boosting the body's immune system.

European herbs and spices :	Thyme, parsley, Basil, Rosemary	Considered beneficial for the body and ideal ingredients to complement sauces, smoothies, and juices.
Essence/ Extracts:	Vanilla, almond, banana, peppermint…	Enhance the flavor of both savory and sweet dishes. However, they should be used in moderation to avoid bitterness and excessive intensity.
Essential oils:	Cinnamon, peppermint, lemongrass, lime peel…	More concentrated than essence/extract, making them more expensive. Due to their concentrated nature, only a minimal amount is required to avoid overpowering other flavors. Approximately one drop can replace a teaspoon of herbal seasoning.

BITTERNESS AND SPICE IN COOKING
Aromatic and Flavorful Ingredients:

Onion Varieties	Onions come in various forms, including shallots, scallions, leeks, and more. They add depth and flavor to a wide range of dishes.
Garlic	Garlic can be used fresh or in powdered form. Using garlic powder reduces its pungency while retaining its flavor. It's known for its natural antibiotic properties and anti-inflammatory benefits.
Ginger	Ginger is ideal for cold climates and offers improved digestion and immune-boosting properties. Its unique flavor can enhance both sweet and savory dishes.
Chilli	Chili peppers, including goat horn pepper, bird's eye chili, and capsicum annum, add spiciness and tantalize the taste buds. While spicy is not one of the 5 basic flavors, it contributes to the deliciousness of dishes.
Pepper Varieties	• Black Pepper: Known for its distinctive aroma and spiciness, black pepper can be used whole, coarsely ground, or as powder. • White Pepper (Peppercorn): Slightly less aromatic than black pepper but still spicy, white pepper maintains its spiciness. • Fresh Pepper: In its fresh form, it provides a mild and highly fragrant spiciness, making it great for salads and garnishing.
Mustard	• Green Mustard (Wasabi): Made from horseradish, green mustard has a strong and spicy taste. It's available in both powder and paste form and should be used sparingly. • Yellow Mustard: Made from white mustard seeds mixed with sugar, oil, vinegar, and turmeric, yellow mustard has a milder taste. • Dijon Mustard: Dijon mustard is made from brown mustard mixed with wine, offering a unique flavor profile. These aromatic ingredients not only add flavor but also bring a depth of character to your culinary creations. Experimenting with these ingredients can lead to exciting and diverse dishes.

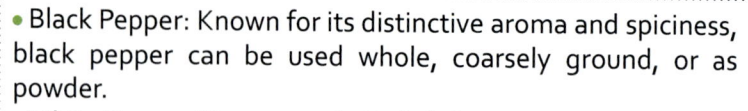

Lesson 10: Umami flavor

In Japanese, 'umami' translates to 'the essence of deliciousness,' a concept first identified in Japan. This unique flavor was named 'umami' by Dr. Kikunae Ikeda while he was studying the Dashi broth, traditionally made from kombu seaweed. He recognized a distinct taste that differed from the four basic tastes already known. Umami has several notable characteristics:

- It spreads across the surface of the tongue.
- It lingers longer than other tastes.
- It stimulates the taste buds and increases saliva production.

Seaweed	Nori Seaweed
Fermented Foods	Tamari Miso Kimchi Nutritional yeast
Vegetables	Sun-dried tomatoes, sun-dried mushrooms, red pumpkin

Lesson 11 Fat

OIL

Peanut oil 	Cold-pressed peanut oil is known for promoting heart health, alleviating constipation, and boosting the immune system
Coconut oil 	This oil is rich in vitamins, minerals, and has potent anti-inflammatory properties. Its distinctive, strong flavor might not suit everyone's taste.
Sesame oil 	Opt for cold-pressed, artisanal sesame oil for its richness in beneficial fats, vitamins, and minerals, particularly iron and calcium. It's also used in oil pulling for body detoxification.
Olive oil 	A great source of Omega-3 and Omega-6, olive oil is beneficial for the heart and nervous system. It's ideal for drizzling over salads and creating various sauces.
Other oils 	Include cold-pressed oils from seeds like walnuts, almonds, and flaxseeds avocado oil (pressed from avocado seeds) and grape seed oil.

SEEDS

Cashews, almonds, walnuts, and macadamias enrich dips, spreads, and sauces with their rich flavors.

FRUITS

Avocado	Their creamy and mildly neutral flavor, and young coconut meat are versatile ingredients in raw vegan dishes.
Coconut	Young coconut meat

Lesson 12 — Binding agents

Irish moss 	Usage: Irish moss serves as a natural binder in raw vegan recipes such as jellies, cakes, ice creams, and cheeses. It offers a softer texture than agar. Taste: It has a slight seaweed-like taste, so it's best used in moderation. Preparation: The fresh variety requires soaking for 30 minutes to 1 hour. Dried Irish moss needs thorough rinsing to remove any dirt or saltiness, followed by soaking for 6-8 hours. Storage Tip: Blend Irish moss with water and pour it into trays to form cubes. These can be refrigerated for up to a week or frozen for 3-4 months.
Xanthan gum 	Xanthan gum is a vegan-friendly thickening agent. It's produced through the fermentation of polysaccharides by specific bacteria. In raw vegan cuisine, xanthan gum adds thickness and consistency to soups, sauces, and gluten-free baked goods. It enhances texture and stability without altering the flavor.
Psyllium Husk 	Psyllium husk is known for its high fiber content, which aids in intestinal cleansing. It's effective in binding and thickening liquid mixtures in various raw vegan dishes.

Notes

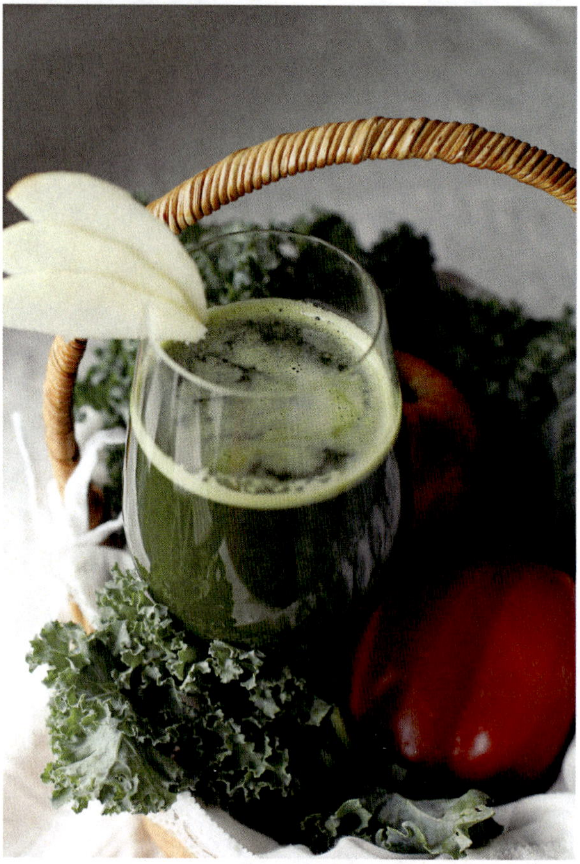
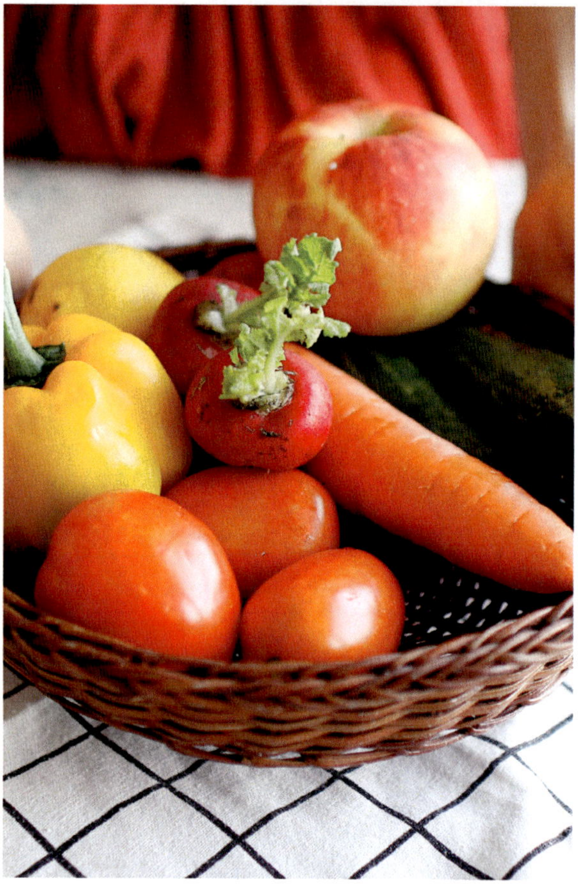

part 3

FOOD HANDLING AND PRESERVATION

Lesson 13 — Fruits

Some fruits undergo a post-harvest ripening process, where their flavors and textures continue to develop, reaching peak deliciousness even after being picked. This characteristic is crucial for determining the ideal time to consume these fruits for optimal taste and nutritional value. On the other hand, certain fruits must be harvested only when they are fully ripe on the plant, as they do not mature or improve in quality after being picked. Understanding this difference is key to enjoying most fruits when they offer the best flavor and nutritional benefits.

Bananas	Available in green, semi-ripe, and fully ripe stages. Use fully ripe bananas (with brown spots) for smoothies and baking. For storage, peel and freeze them
Apples	They don't ripen after harvest. Store them in the fridge or dehydrate for long-term use.
Pears	They continue to ripen post-harvest. Once ripe, store in a cool place or sun-dry.
Citrus fruits	Includes lime, orange, tangerine, and grapefruit. They don't ripen after being picked (except limes). Store at room temperature or refrigerate. If storing in the fridge, take out and leave the fruits at room temperature before using to enhance the sweetness. Use the citrus peel for skin exfoliation.

Stone fruits   	Peaches and Plums: Let them ripen at room temperature; they are ready when slightly soft at the top. Refrigerate for storage. Remove pits and the fresh can be frozen or sun-dried. Cherries: Harvest when fully ripe, as they won't ripen further. Store in the fridge to maintain freshness. Mangoes: Harvest ripe, then allow to ripen further at room temperature.
Watermelons 	For freshness, cut into slices and store in the freezer.
Berries  	Strawberries: Best when locally grown and ripe; freeze for storage. Blueberries: Rinse only before eating; can also be frozen or dried. Cranberries: Dried cranberries are a good purchase option.
Avocados 	Ripen faster in a paper bag due to ethylene gas. Store ripe avocados in the refrigerator.

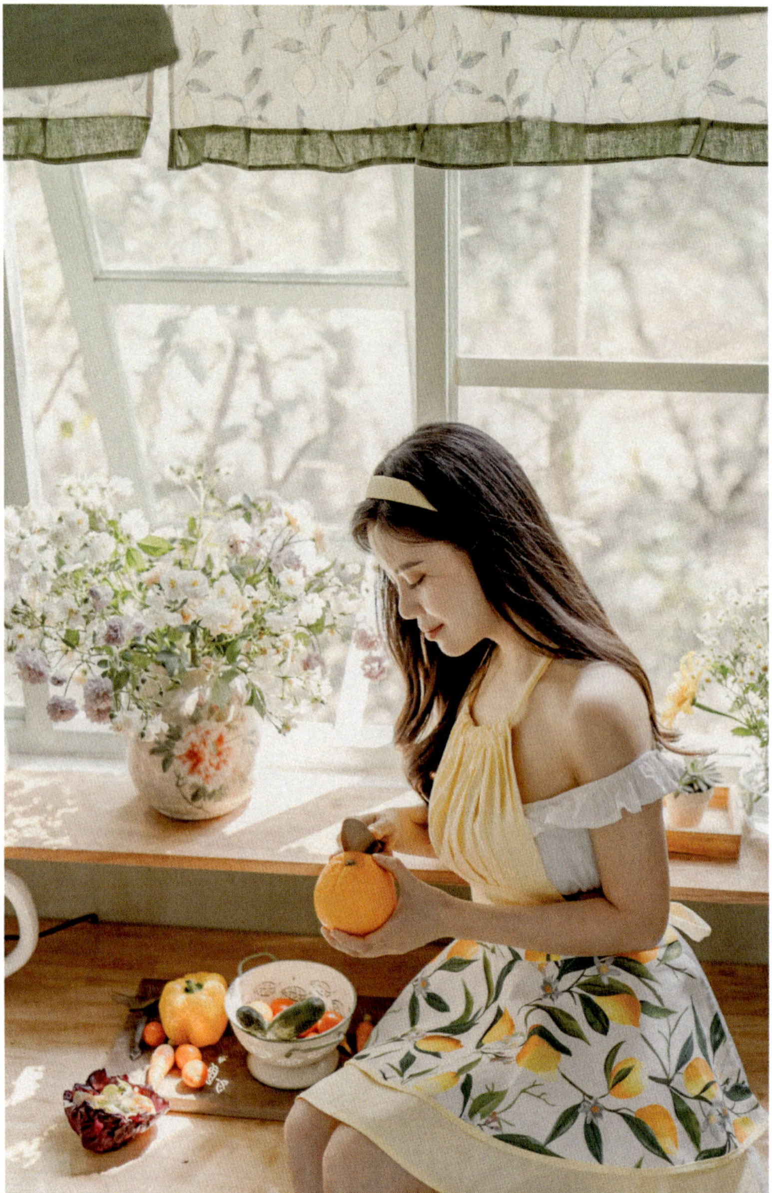

Lesson 14 — Vegetables

Onions	It's important to avoid storing onions alongside potatoes, as the gases released by onions can lead to undesirable sprouting in potatoes. However, storing onions near garlic is perfectly fine. If you wish to lessen the pungency of onions, consider soaking them in saltwater for a duration of 30 minutes to 1 hour.
Tomatoes	The majority of commercially grown tomatoes are harvested while still green and left to ripen on their own, resulting in a bland taste. The research reports that lycopene a component in tomatoes, is better absorbed when cooked When machine-processed, the cell wall is broken down for easier absorption. Avoid refrigerating tomatoes as the cold temperature can make them mushy due to the starch content. If there are leftover cut tomatoes, store them in a cool section of the refrigerator. Sun-dried tomatoes can be used to create a sauce.

Green leafy vegetables 	• Store in a zip bag or air tight containers. • Avoid washing before storage, as it can increase moisture content and lead to rapid deterioration. If preparing for the next day's meal, ensure the greens are thoroughly dry after washing. • Leafy greens with a deep green color can be refrigerated as they prefer colder temperatures, while sprouts are best kept in a slightly cooler environment.
Bell peppers 	Available in green, red, and yellow, but avoid buying green as these are unripe bell peppers. Mature bell peppers break from their green state to red, yellow, or orange. Many find it challenging to digest raw green bell peppers, so it's advisable to opt for ripe ones.

Lesson 15

Nuts and seeds

- To ensure optimal preservation, it's crucial to protect the nuts from air, light, and humidity.

- The best way to store them is in a cool, dry environment. This is particularly important for nuts rich in unsaturated fatty acids, like cashews and macadamias, which can degrade at room temperature. In tropical climates, where heat and humidity are prevalent, improper storage can lead to spoilage, infestations, and mold.

- For longer shelf life, consider storing the nuts in a ziplock bag and placing them in the freezer. This method helps in retaining their freshness and preventing rancidity.

- In cases where freezer space is limited, a viable alternative is to keep them in airtight glass or plastic containers, stored in a cool and dark place, away from direct sunlight and heat sources.

- If the nuts have a higher oil content and appear oily, you can extend their freshness by either sun-drying them or using a gentle heat-drying method at about 45 degrees Celsius. This process reduces their moisture content, thereby prolonging their shelf life and maintaining their nutritional quality.

- To ensure optimal preservation, it's crucial to protect the nuts from air, light, and humidity.

Notes

part

4

Knife skills

Lesson 16 — Types of knives

Chef's knife: Knife used in both Western and Asian kitchens.	Multipurpose Can opt for a type with small, anti-stick dimples
Paring Knife	Peel Slice small foods.
Serrated Knife	Cut tough outer skin while maintaining a soft interior, suitable for tomatoes and sushi.
Bird's Beak Paring Knife	Peel in a swift, continuous spiral for fruits like apples, kiwis, mangoes.
Cleaver	Open coconut husks
Wave Knife	Slice vegetables and fruits.
Pastry Knife	Dough Scraper Palette knife Offset palette knife Serrated/non-serrated cake knife.
Grater	Grate hard vegetables into small pieces (carrots, ginger, taro...). Grate orange/lemon

Lesson 17: Choosing and maintaining knives

- Sharp knives: Avoid accidents. Dull knives are more prone to slipping and accidents than sharp ones.

- Avoid dishwasher cleaning. Minimize the use of dishwashing water and chemicals.

- Avoid using the knife tip to open cans as it may cause damage.

- Do not sharpen ceramic knives or serrated knives.

- Sharping tools
Honing rod
Sharpening stone
Roller sharp: knife sharpening tool

Lesson 18: Choosing cutting board

	WOODEN BOARDS	**PLASTIC BOARDS**
Advantages	Less bacterial retention due to bacteria sinking deeper into the wood surface, making it less conducive to bacterial growth (according to research by Professor Dean O. Cliver, University of California).	More prone to bacterial retention even after thorough cleaning.
Disadvantages	Heavier More expensive	Lightweight and cost-effective

Note.

Use Separate Cutting Boards: Foods derived from animals tend to have a higher risk of bacterial contamination compared to plant-based foods. However, in many households, both animal-based and vegan dishes are prepared, often on the same cutting board. To minimize the risk of cross-contamination, it is advisable to use separate cutting boards for these two food categories. In situations where separate boards aren't available, designate different sides of the same board for animal products and plant-based ingredients. Additionally, for those using a dedicated vegan cutting board, it's a good practice to further differentiate sections of the board, for example, using one side for strong-smelling ingredients like garlic, onions, and ginger, to prevent their aromas from transferring to more delicate fruits and vegetables.

Securing the Cutting Board: For safe and efficient chopping, it's essential to have a stable cutting surface. This can be achieved by placing a damp cloth underneath the cutting board. This simple step prevents the board from sliding, reducing the risk of accidents and ensuring more precise cuts.

Lesson 19
Knife grip and cutting technique

Holding the Knife: Use the 'chef's grip'. Hold the handle with your dominant hand, with your thumb and the side of your index finger gripping the blade just above the handle. This provides control and precision.

Supporting Hand Technique: Use the 'claw grip' with your non-dominant hand. Tuck your fingertips under, so the knuckles are forward, forming a guide for the knife. This keeps your fingers safe and helps in making uniform cuts.

It's crucial to practice these techniques for safety and efficiency in the kitchen. The chef's grip on the knife offers stability and control, while the claw grip helps in maintaining consistent cuts and protects the fingers.

1. Knife Grip and Cutting Technique:
Refer to the correct knife grip and cutting technique in the images: holding the knife and supporting hand.

2. Raw Vegan Cutting Skills:

Brunoise

Julienne

Batonnet

Diced

COOKING RECIPE
Menu

Sample menu 1

	Monday	Tuesday	Wednesday	Thursday	Friday	Saturday	Sunday
BREAKFAST	Fruit Juice Truffle protein	Fruit Juice Apple Muffin	Fruit Juice Truffle protein	Fruit Juice "Omelette"	Fruit Juice Avocado Porridge	Fruit Juice Apple Muffin	Fruit Juice "Omelette"
MORNING SNACK	Vegan Yogurt	Green Smoothie	Kale Chips	Fresh Fruit	Vegan Yogurt	Green Smoothie	Kale Chips
LUNCH	Russian Salad	Carrot Soup	Sushi maki	Russian Salad	Mixed Noodles	Carrot Soup	Beetroot ravioli
AFTERNOON SNACK	Apple tortilla	Plant-based milk	Chewy-Dried Fruit	Brownies	Plant-based milk	Chewy-Dried Fruit	Green Smoothie
DINNER	"Zucchini" noodles	Orange apricot mint salad	"Zucchini" noodles	Banana blossom salad	Orange apricot mint salad	Sushi maki	Banana blossom salad

Sample menu 2

	Monday	Tuesday	Wednesday	Thursday	Friday	Saturday	Sunday
BREAKFAST	Fruit Juice Carrot Walnut Cookies	Fruit Juice Tomato Soup	Fruit Juice Banana Coconut Pancakes	Fruit Juice Carrot Walnut Cookies	Fruit Juice Kohlrabi dumplings	Fruit Juice Banana Coconut Pancakes	Fruit Juice Kohlrabi dumplings
MORNING SNACK	Perilla snack	Green smoothie	Perilla chips	Plant-based milk	Green smoothie	Yogurt	Plant-based milk
LUNCH	Zero waste patties	Burger	Pomelo salad	Kale salad with avocado and coconut dressing	Zero waste patties	Burger	Beetroot ravioli
AFTERNOON SNACK	Chewy-Dried Fruit	Mango mousse cake	Coconut ice cream	Chewy-Dried Fruit	Fruit cheese-cake	Fresh fruit	Coconut ice cream
DINNER	Papaya salad with Thai tamarind sauce	Tomato soup	Mac n cheese	Fish Cake	Pumpkin curry soup	Kale salad with cashew dressing	Fish Cake

53

Notes

Part 5

FERMENTED FOOD PRODUCTION

Lesson 20: VEGAN YOGURT

Ingredients: Makes 10-12 small jars of yogurt

100 grams of cashews, soaked overnight

100gr young coconut meat

10 dates

500 ml filtered water

1 vanilla pod (or 1 teaspoon vanilla extract)

1/2 teaspoon vegan yogurt starter (about 1.5-2 grams depending on type)

Instructions:

- Sterilize the yogurt cup with boiling water and drain (or use a sterilizer).
- Wash the cashews and drain
- Put cashews, dates, young coconut meat, vanilla and filtered water into a blender and blend until the cashews are completely smooth, strain if necessary).
- Once the milk is smooth, add the vegan yogurt starter and pulse for a few seconds to dissolve in the milk (vegan yogurt starter is only needed for the first batch. Next time, keep a cup of yogurt as seed culture).
- Pour the mixture into prepared yogurt cups, optionally cover with lids.
- Place the cups in a large pot/tray, covered with a cloth. Keep them at room temperature for 8-12 hours. Check until the yogurt thickens and tastes sour
- Seal the yogurt cups with lids and store them in the refrigerator, saving 1 cup for the next time. Subsequent batches of yogurt will become flavorful over time

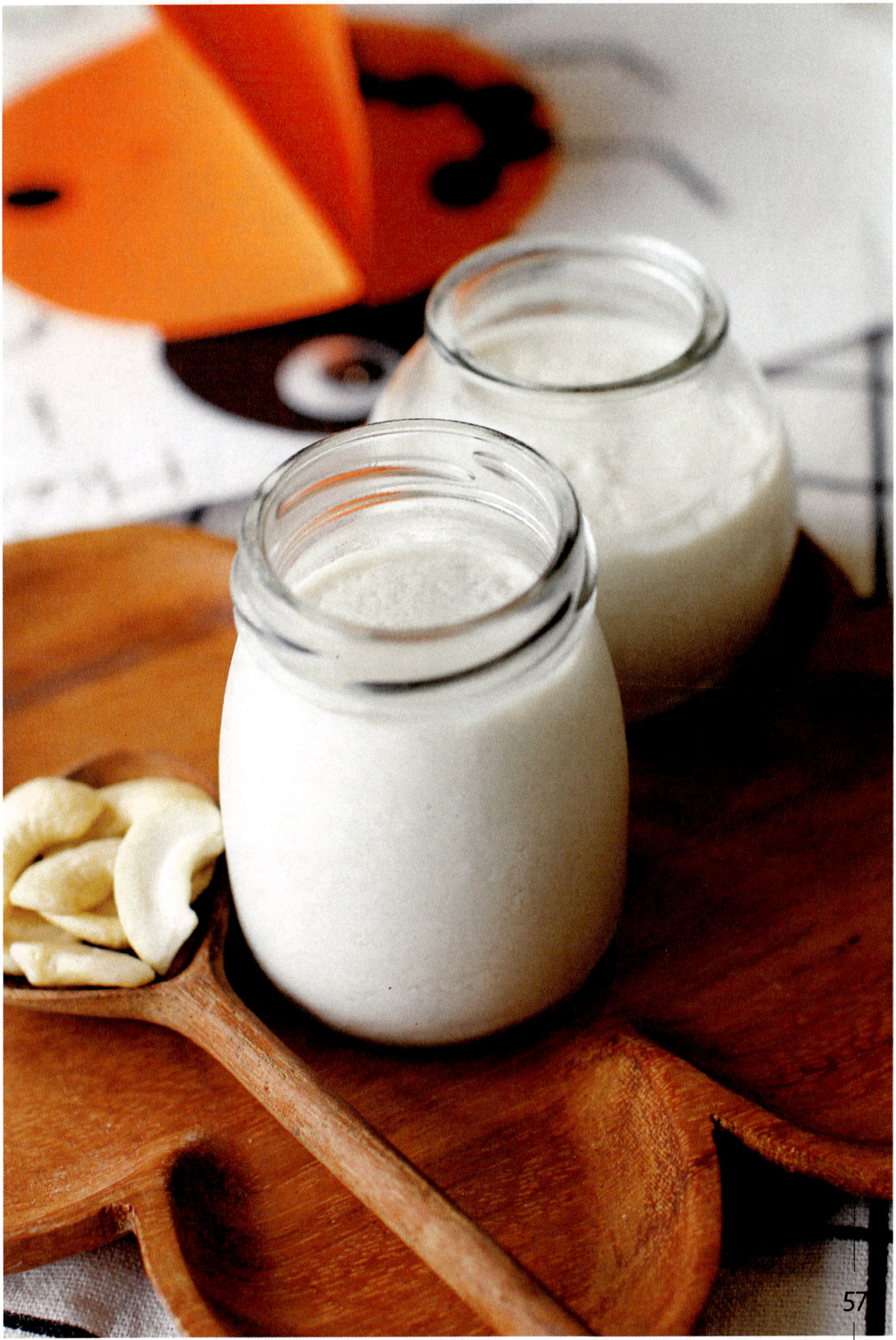

Lesson 21: VEGAN CHEESE

Ingredients: 4 servings

250 grams cashews (about 2 cups), soaked for 4-6 hours. Wash and discard water

400 ml filtered water (about 2 cups)

1 tablespoon miso paste

2 tablespoons nutritional yeast

1 tablespoon apple cider vinegar

4 dates

50 grams Irish moss (soak for at least 30 minutes then wash thoroughly to clean and remove saltiness, should be soaked overnight)

1/4 teaspoon vegan culture (can use vegan yogurt culture or cultures labeled as cultured kefir or probiotic starter for the first time. Next time, keep a part of the cheese as starter culture similar to yogurt).

Instructions

- Blend all ingredients in a blender.

- Pour mixture into a glass container, cover it with cloth and let it ferment for 6-8 hours, taste to see if it has reached acidity.

- Store in the refrigerator and preserve for 15-20 days.

- Keep approximately 1/2 cup of cheese as a glaze for future use

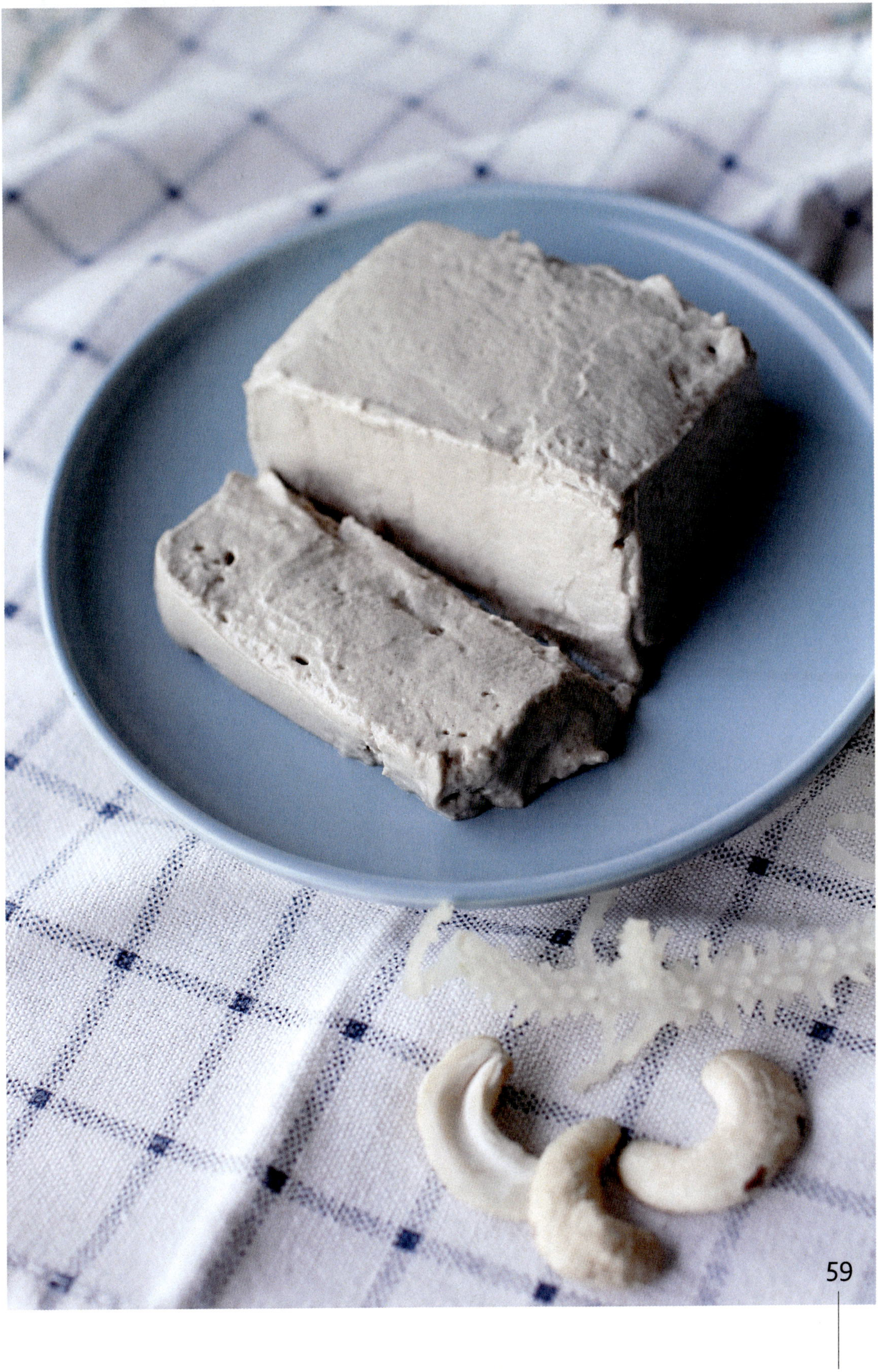

Lesson 22: NUTRIENT-RICH KIMCHI

Ingredients

1kg napa cabbage (about 1 large head)

250g daikon radish, sliced/stripped (about 1 medium-sized)

150g carrots, sliced/stripped (about 1 large carrot)

25g spring onion/chives

Coarse salt for brining

Kimchi Sauce

5g ginger

5g garlic

3 goat horn peppers (or 1-2 tablespoons chili powder)

1/2 onion

1/2 apple

1/2 pear

15g vegan fish sauce

15g rock sugar/brown sugar

Note

Either apples or pears can be used, choose one.

If you prefer a milder taste, substitute chili powder with red bell peppers.

Instructions

- Cut the large cabbage vertically into 6 pieces (4 for a small cabbage).

- Soak the cabbage in water, rubbing salt between the leaves. Let it sit for 1 hour.

- Drain and squeeze out water, repeat 4 times. Set aside.

Blend the sauce ingredients until smooth. Coat the cabbage leaves evenly.

- Layer in a container: cabbage, spring onion/chives, repeat. Top with carrots and radishes.

- Leave it outside for 5-6 hours. Taste, and if satisfied, refrigerate.

Note: When you want to consume your ferment quickly, opt for brown sugar. However, for a slower fermentation process, choose rock sugar instead, as it ferments at a slower rate compared to brown sugar.

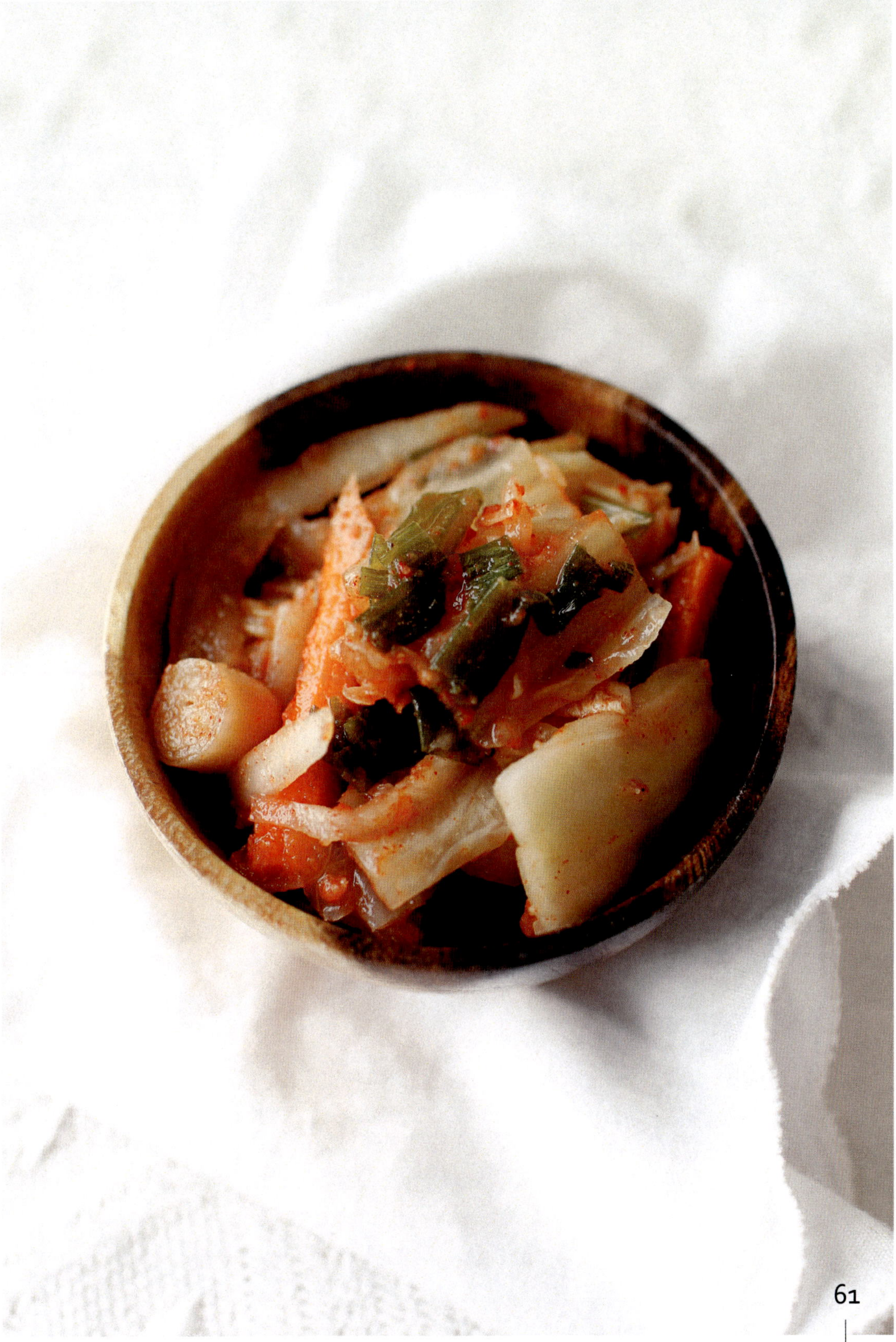

Lesson 23: PICKLED VEGETABLES WITH ENRICHED PROBIOTICS

Korean Radish Pickles with Enriched Probiotics

Ingredients

2 radishes, sliced into rounds or sticks

100g brown sugar

100g apple cider vinegar

1 pinch of turmeric powder

Instructions

- Place the radishes in a container.
- Add brown sugar, apple cider vinegar, and a pinch of turmeric.
- Shake the container well to ensure even coating.
- Seal the container and refrigerate for 2-3 days before consumption.
- Store in a cool place and enjoy gradually over 2-3 months.
- Yield: Approximately 4 servings
- Serving Suggestion: These pickled Korean radishes make a delicious side dish or a crunchy topping for salads and sandwiches.

Quick-Pickled Vegetables

Ratio

> 2 water : 1 vinegar : 1 sugar : 0.1 salt

Ingredients

200g jicamas, julienned

100g carrots, julienned

2 tablespoons vinegar

2 tablespoons sugar

4 tablespoons water

1/2 teaspoon salt

Instructions

- Place jicamas and carrots in a double-layered basket with a water-catching feature.

- Mix the seasoning and apply it to the jicamas and carrots, toss evenly.

- After 5-10 minutes, drain excess liquid from the vegetables, and they are ready to be served.

Pickled herb vegetables

Ingredients

1 onion, thinly sliced or julienned

2 tablespoons vinegar

2 tablespoons sugar

4 tablespoons water

1/2 teaspoon salt

2 cloves

1 small cinnamon stick

1 star anise

Instructions

- Mix the pickling ingredients, add the sliced onion, and let it soak for 1-2 days before use

Notes

part

6

BASIC RECIPES

Lesson 24: RAW COCONUT MILK

Coconut milk ratio

2 coconuts : 1 water

Ingredients

400g young coconut meat

200g water

Instructions

- Blend the ingredients until smooth using a high-speed blender or a food processor. If you prefer a smoother texture, strain the mixture through a nut milk bag or cheesecloth.

- Store the coconut milk in an airtight container in the refrigerator for 7-10 days or in a silicone tray in the freezer for 2-3 months.

- Remember to shake or stir the coconut milk if it separates before use.

- Serving Suggestions: Use this homemade raw coconut milk in smoothies, breakfast cereal, cooking, or baking for a creamy and dairy-free addition to your dishes.

Lesson 25

RAW NUT BUTTER

COMMON FORMULA

Seeds
Sesame seeds, black sesame seeds, almonds, walnuts, cashews, macadamia nuts, hazelnuts...

Spices
Salt, cooking oil, sugar

Flavor enhancers
Cocoa powder, vanilla, dried coconut

Nutrient boosters
Cashew seed, pumpkin seeds, almonds, sunflower seeds... finely chopped

Almond Butter

300g almond

2 dates

1 cup almond oil

1 pinch of salt

2 tablespoons chia seeds

- Process the ingredients, excluding chia seeds, until smooth butter is formed.

- Add chia seeds, mix well.

- Store in an airtight container.

67

Tahini

200g white sesame seeds
1/2 - 1 cup sesame oil

Cinnamon Vanilla Cashew Butter

300g cashews
2 dates
1 pinch of salt
1 teaspoon vanilla extract
1 teaspoon ground cinnamon

- Blend ingredients until smooth.
- Store in an airtight container.

Nutella

1 cup hazelnuts, soaked
1/2-1 cup coconut oil
1/4 cup coconut sugar
2 tablespoons cocoa powder
1 teaspoon vanilla extract

- Blend ingredients until smooth. Store in an airtight container.

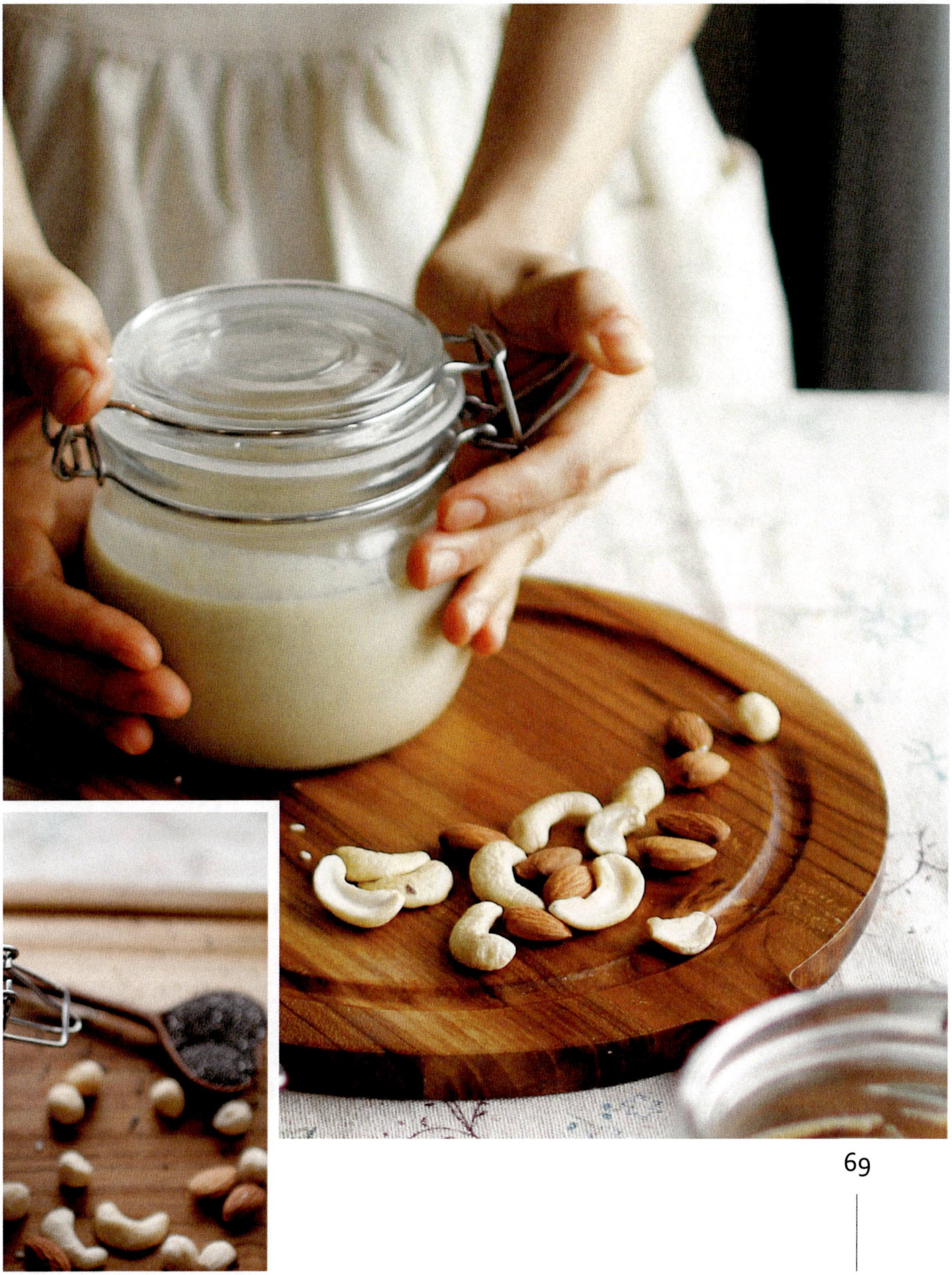

Lesson 26

RAW PLANT-BASED MILKS

COMMON FORMULA

Basic plant-based milk
Cashew, almonds, walnuts, macadamia, pumpkin seeds...

Plant-based milk + vegetables/fruits
Various nuts and additional ingredients such as carrots, pumpkins, zucchini, mangoes, strawberries, bananas...

Sweetening agents
Dates, coconut sugar...

Flavor
Cocoa powder, vanilla, coconut, cinnamon powder, essential oils

Cashew pumpkin seed milk

25g cashews

100g pumpkin

6-8 dates

1 teaspoon vanilla extract

1/2 teaspoon cinnamon powder

1/2 teaspoon nutmeg

1/2 teaspoon ginger powder

500-600ml water

71

Macadamia banana spinach milk

50g macadamia nuts

1 banana

1 handful of spinach

6 dates

1 teaspoon vanilla extract

500-600ml water

Coconut chocolate almond milk

50g almonds

1 teaspoon cocoa powder

5 dates

1 tablespoon coconut milk (see Lesson 24) or 1 piece of young coconut meat

1 teaspoon of vanilla extract

500ml water.

Lesson 27: KETCHUP

Ingredients

2 tomatoes

1 tamarind

5 dates

1/2 teaspoon garlic powder

1/2 teaspoon onion powder

1 pinch of salt

1 pinch of pepper

1 pinch of xanthan gum

Instructions

- Blend all ingredients, excluding xanthan gum, until smooth.
- Add xanthan gum and blend for an additional 30 seconds.
- Store in a cool place for 5-7 days

Notes

Part 7

DEHYDRATION TECHNIQUE

Lesson 28 — APPLE MUFFINS

Ingredients

12 muffins

6-8 dried apricots, chopped (substitute with cranberries if preferred)

1 cup orange juice

40g dates (medium-sized seeds), deseeded

2 apples (or substitute with pears), deseeded and finely grated (350g)

1/2 zucchini, finely grated

1 banana (90g)

1/2 cup almond flour

1/2 cup finely chopped almonds

1/2 cup flaxseed meal

1 vanilla pod (or 1 teaspoon vanilla extract)

1 lemonade zest of one lemon

Instructions

- Begin by soaking the dried apricots and dates in orange juice for a minimum of 15 minutes. After soaking, remove the apricots and keep them aside.

- Next, blend the orange juice, soaked dates, banana, and flaxseed until you achieve a smooth and silky mixture.

- Combine this mixture with the set-aside ingredients, then dehydrate for 12 to 24 hours. At 12 hours, you'll notice the cake has set yet retains a soft structure. For a firmer texture, continue the dehydration process.

77

Lesson 29: CARROT WALNUT COOKIES

Ingredients

4-6 servings

100g oats

120g almond flour

120g grated carrots (about 1 medium-sized carrot)

50g raisins

60g chopped walnuts

50ml olive oil/almond oil

2 teaspoons (5g) ginger powder

2 teaspoons cinnamon powder

1 teaspoon cardamom powder (optional)

1 pinch of salt

50g coconut blossom nectar/ maple syrup/blended date (optional)

Instructions

- First, use a food processor to grind the oats and almond into a fine powder. Then, thoroughly mix all the ingredients together.

- Using a tablespoon for measurement, portion out the mixture, shape it into rounds, and then flatten each piece.

- Dehydrate the shaped rounds for 2 hours in a dehydrator, or alternatively, bake them in an oven set to 45 degrees Celsius. Once done, store them in an airtight container kept in a cool place; they should remain fresh for 7 to 10 days.

Note: Oats can be replaced with almond flour for 100% raw.

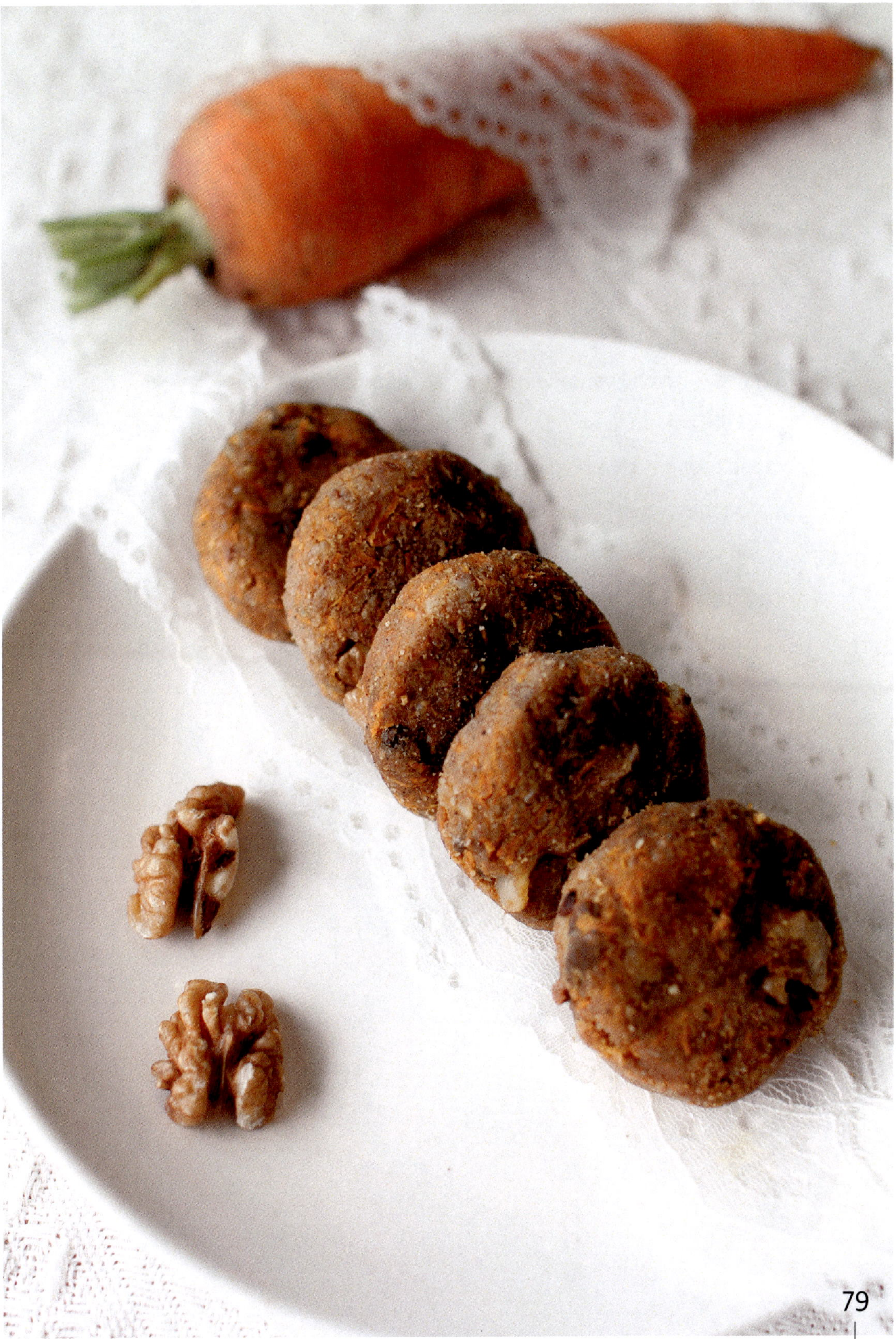

Lesson 30: BANANA COCONUT CHIA SEED PANCAKES

Ingredients

Makes 6-8 small pancakes

1/2 cup almond flour

2 tablespoons chia seeds

2 bananas

120g young coconut meat

1/4 cup water

1 teaspoon cinnamon

1 teaspoon vanilla extract

2 tablespoons goji berries

Instructions

- Blend bananas, coconut meat, cinnamon, and vanilla until smooth. Mix with the remaining ingredients.

- Spoon 2 tablespoons of batter onto a silicone-lined baking sheet. Dehydrate at 45°C for 2 hours, then flip and dehydrate for an additional 10 hours.

81

Lesson 31 — "OMELETTE"

Ingredients: 2 servings

1 zucchini (approximately 300g)

100g avocado

1/2 cup cashews (about 60g), soaked for 2 hours

2 tablespoons nutritional yeast

1 tablespoon coconut sugar

1/2 teaspoon paprika powder

1/2 teaspoon onion powder

1/2 teaspoon Indian black salt (optional, but adds an egg-like flavor)

1 pinch of pink salt (if skipping Indian black salt, increase pink salt to 1/2 teaspoon)

1 pinch of turmeric powder (optional)

2 tablespoons psyllium husk

Instructions

- Process all ingredients in a food processor

- Dehydrator: Spread the mixture on a dehydrator tray lined with parchment paper, dehydrate at 45°C for 12 hours, then flip and dehydrate for an additional 4-5 hours. You can also use an oven or air fryer.

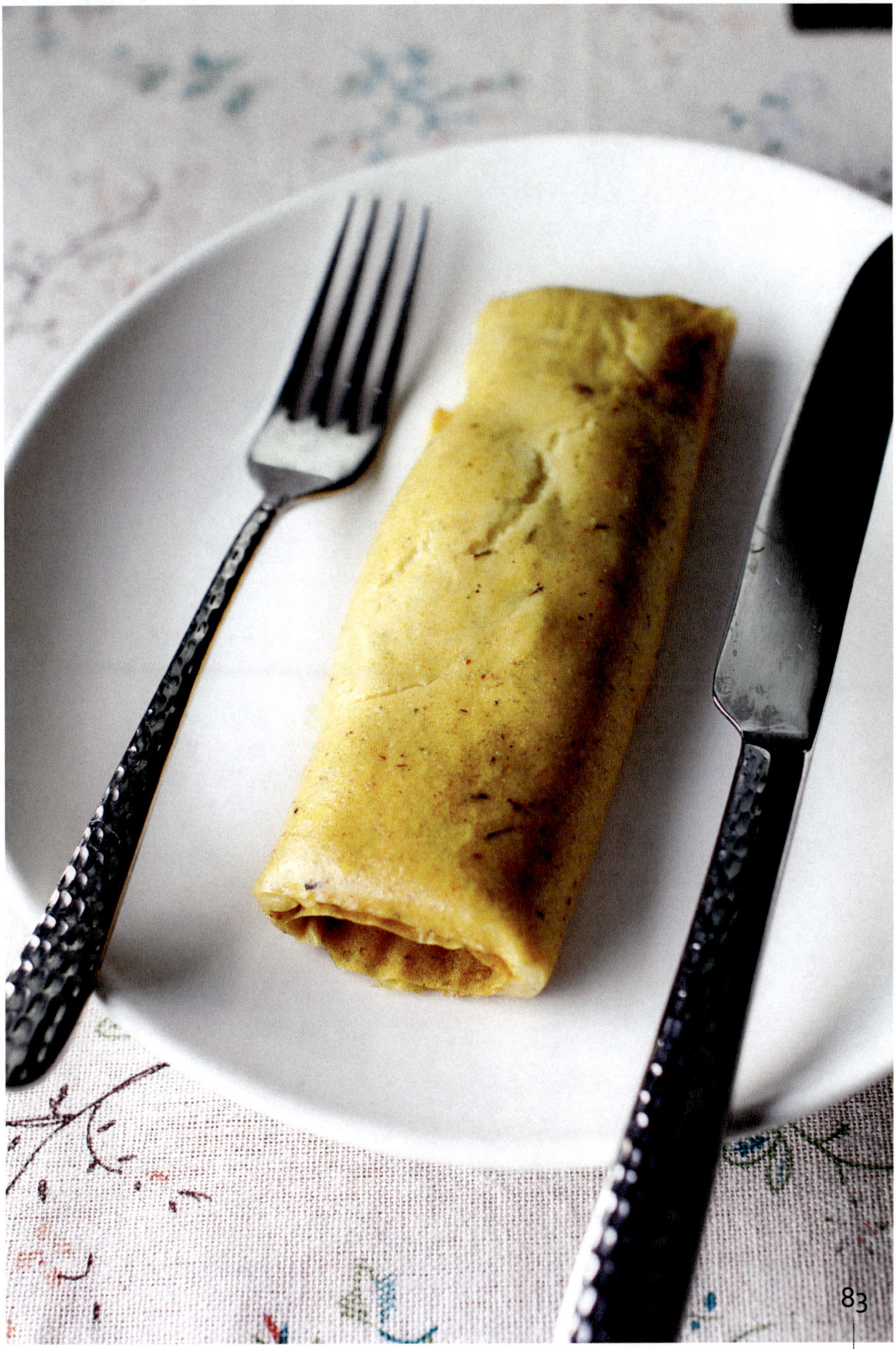

Lesson 32: ZERO WASTE PATTIES

Ingredients: 3-4 servings

pulp of 1 carrot and 2 jicamas (or 1/2 fresh carrot + 1 fresh jicama)

180g avocado (about 1/2 large or 1 small)

1/4 cup chopped cashews (or almonds)

50g Irish moss, soaked and finely chopped

1 lemongrass stalk, finely minced

A handful of coriander, finely chopped

1 stalk of green onions, finely chopped.

1/2 teaspoon garlic powder

1/2 teaspoon onion powder

1 tablespoon vegan fish sauce

1 tablespoon white sesame seeds

Instructions

- Grate the jicamas and carrots, ensuring to separate and reserve the liquid for regular consumption, as it is not needed in this recipe. Use only the pulp. If you're working with fresh jicamas and carrots, finely chop them or use a small grinder. After chopping, be sure to squeeze out any excess water from the jicamas.

- In a separate bowl, mash the avocado until it achieves a smooth consistency.

- Proceed by adding all the remaining ingredients to the bowl containing the mashed avocado. Mix everything thoroughly to ensure a uniform blend.

- Using a tablespoon, scoop out portions of the mixture, shaping each into a patty. Gently press each patty to flatten it.

- Place the patties in a dehydrator set to 45 degrees Celsius and dehydrate for 3-4 hours.

- These zero waste patties are a nutritious and sustainable option that makes the most of ingredients while reducing waste. Enjoy them as a healthy snack or meal option.

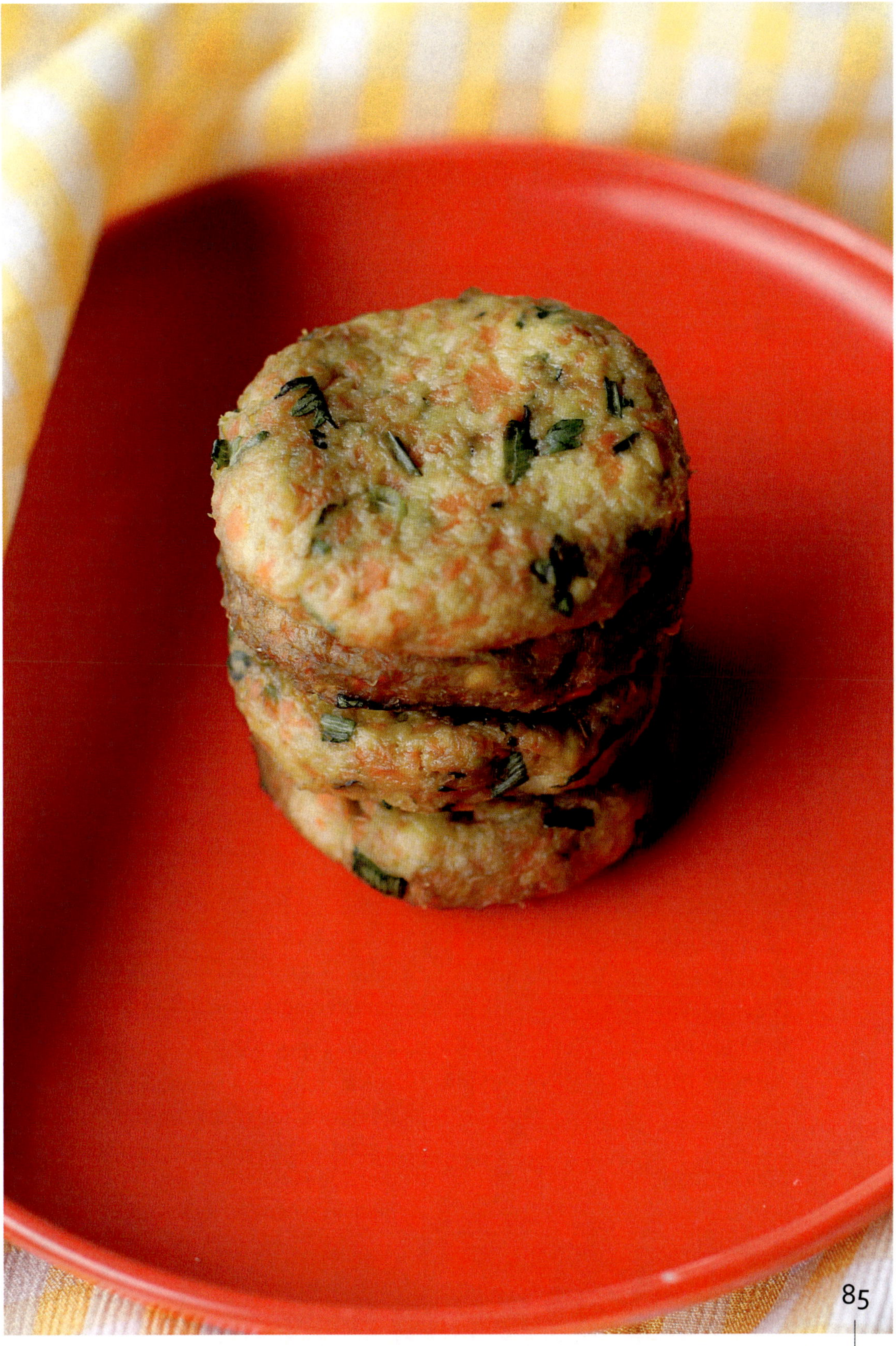

Lesson 33 — "FISH" CAKE

Ingredients: 2-3 servings

1 cup macadamia nuts, 1/2 ground, 1/2 coarsely chopped

150g bell pepper (about 1 medium-sized)

50g Irish moss, soaked for 30 minutes and thoroughly rinsed

2 sheets nori seaweed

1/4 cup finely chopped dill

3-4 stalks of green onions, finely chopped

2 tablespoons nutritional yeast

1 tablespoon onion powder

1 tablespoon garlic powder

1/2 teaspoon cayenne pepper (or smoked paprika)

1/2 teaspoon chili powder (optional for extra spiciness)

Serving Suggestions:
Pineapple
Green bananas
Bean sprouts
Mixed herbs: mint, perilla, elsholtzia

Dipping Sauce:

2 tablespoons water

1 tablespoon coconut sugar (or coconut blossom nectar)

1 tablespoon apple cider vinegar

1 tablespoon vegan fish sauce

Instructions

- Prepare a food processor and add 1/2 portion of macadamia nuts, bell pepper, Irish moss, nutritional yeast, and spices. Blend until smooth. Mix with additional Irish moss and chopped maccamadia for texture.

- Take 2 tablespoons of the mixture and shape into flat rounds.

- Dehydrate at 45 degrees for 5-6 hours.

- Serve directly, either with salad or rolled with lettuce and complementary ingredients.

- These "fish" cakes are a delicious and sustainable alternative to traditional fish cakes, making them a great addition to your plant-based diet. Enjoy them with your favorite dipping sauce and fresh vegetables.

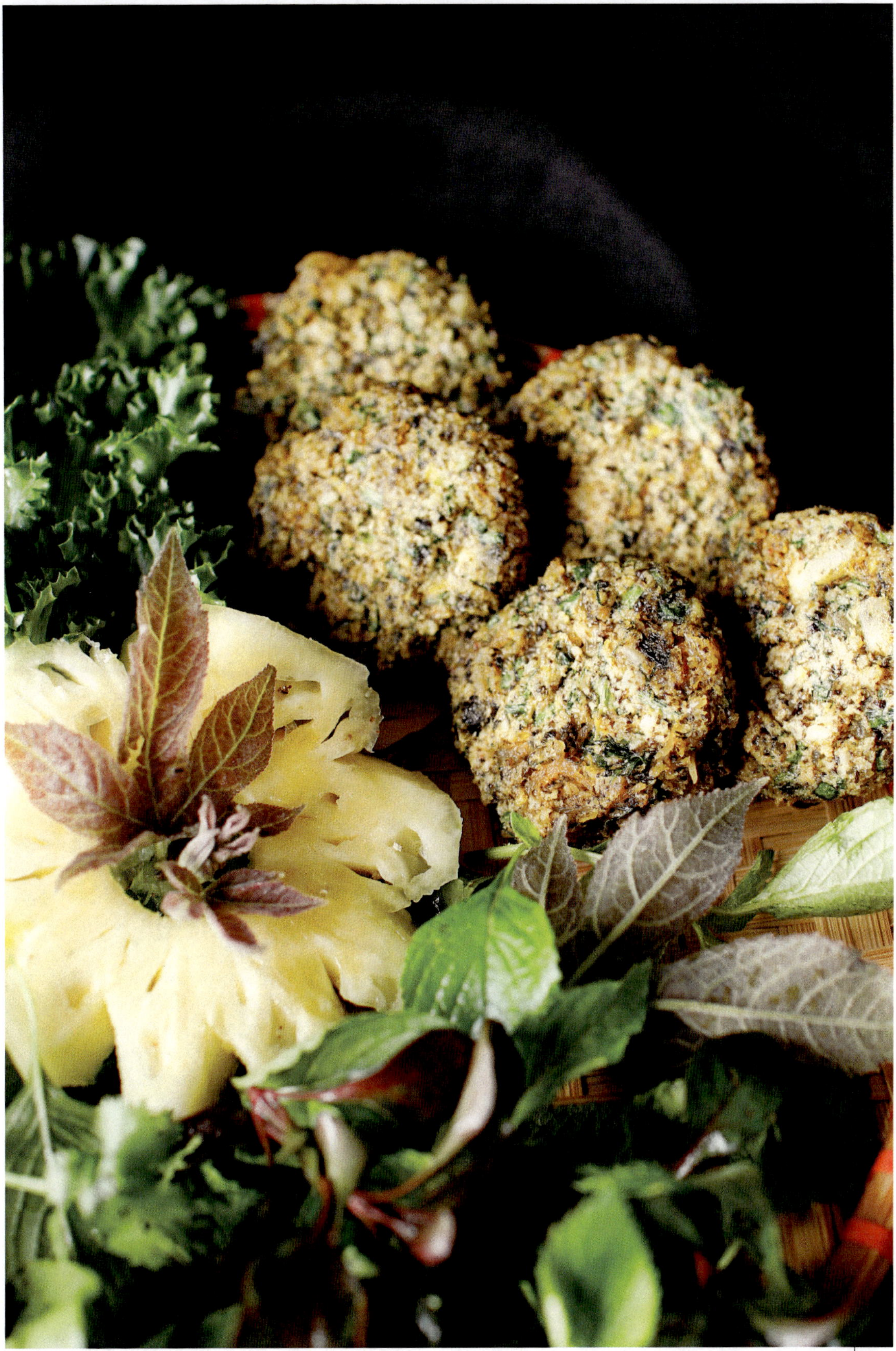

Lesson 34: BURGER

Ingredients: 4-5 patties

1 cup sunflower seeds, soaked overnight
1/2 cup almonds, soaked overnight
160g zucchini
80g beetroot
80g avocado
2 dates
1 teaspoon olive oil
1 teaspoon parsley
1/2 teaspoon paprika powder
1/4 teaspoon salt
1/2 teaspoon garlic powder
1/2 teaspoon onion powder
1 pinch of pepper

Serving Suggestions
Lettuce
Sliced tomatoes
Pickled onions (Lesson 23)

Instructions

- Finely chop all ingredients in a food processor until the mixture becomes sticky.

- Shape into flat, round patties.

- Dehydrate at 45 degrees for 4 hours, then flip and dehydrate for an additional 2 hours.

- Serve with lettuce, tomatoes, and soaked onions.

- These homemade burgers are a healthy and flavorful alternative to traditional meat burgers. Enjoy them with your favorite toppings for a delicious plant-based meal.

Lesson 35: KALE SNACK / PERILLA

Ingredients: 3-4 servings

5-6 curly kale leaves or 200g of perilla

1 cup walnuts, soaked overnight

1/2 cup nutritional yeast

1/4 cup maple leaf syrup

2 tablespoons lemon juice

1 pinch of salt

1/2 teaspoon chili powder (optional for spiciness)

Instructions

- Begin by removing the stems from the curly kale (if using) and discarding them. Wash the kale leaves thoroughly, then allow them to air dry or gently pat them dry with a towel. If you are using perilla leaves, rinse them well and let them dry.
- Next, take the walnuts and wash them once more. Blend these walnuts in a blender with all the other ingredients, except for the kale or perilla leaves.
- Once blended, pour the mixture into a bowl. Take the kale or perilla leaves and massage the mixture into them, ensuring they are well coated.
- Finally, place the coated kale or perilla in a dehydrator and let them dehydrate overnight, which should take about 8-10 hours.
- These crispy kale or perilla snacks make for a delicious and nutritious treat. Enjoy their crunchy texture and flavorful coating as a healthy snack option.

Lesson 36
CHEWY- DRIED FRUIT

Fruits	Preparation	Drying Time
Apple/Pear	Circular slices	3-4h
Pineapple	Circular slices	10-12h
Peach	Remove seeds, slice/piece	10-12h
Mango	Strips	8-10h
Tomato	Sliced	8-10h

91

Part 8

DETOX JUICE

Selecting the Right Juicer Based on Food Type:
1. Centrifugal Juicer: Ideal for quick extraction, but less efficient in terms of juice volumn. It may not extract the maximum amount of vitamins. Generally, these juicers are more suitable for fruits than for leafy greens.
2. Cold-pressed juicer: Operates with minimal heat generation, extracting more pulp and retaining a higher vitamin content. Certain models are versatile, capable of making ice cream, pate, and other foods.

Cleaning Process for Fruits and Vegetables:
1. Soak the fruits and vegetables in salted water for 5 to 10 minutes.
2. After soaking, rinse them one final time using filtered water.

80:20 Principle
80% vegetables
20% fruit

Bitter flavor	Sweet flavor	Sour/sweet sour flavor	Aromatic flavor
Celery	Cucumber	Orange	Coriander
Kale	Carrot	Lemon	Parsley
Spinach	Jicamas	Pineapple	Ginger
Rainbow chard	Bell pepper	Grapefruit	Peppermint
Dandelion	Beetroot	Passion fruit	Mint
White radish/ red radish	Apple	Starfruit	Lemongrass
Purple cabbage	Pear	Tomato	
Wheatgrass	Watermelon		
Broccoli	Guava		
Pennywort	Honeydew melon		
	Grapes		
	Pomegranate		

Lesson 37
GOLDEN SUN JUICE

Ingredients

400g yellow bell peppers (approximately 2 medium-sized peppers)

500g pineapple (approximately 1 medium-sized pineapple)

1/4 lime

2 cucumbers

Lesson 38

DETOX JUICE

Ingredients

200g celery
1/2 grapefruit
1 carrot
2 cucumbers
A handful of cilantro

Lesson 39
VIOLET GUARDIAN JUICE

Ingredients

200g purple cabbage (about 1/2 large cabbage or 1 small cabbage)

500g jicama (2 small-sized jicama)

2 Guavas

Lesson 40: RED ENERGY JUICE

Ingredients

150g spinach

200g beetroot (approximately 2 medium-sized beetroots)

2 small red radish (about 30g)

300g watermelon

1 handful of peppermint

Lesson 41
ANTI-INFLAMMATORY JUICE

Ingredients

200g dandelion
200g pumpkin
300g cantaloupe
2 oranges
1/2 stalk lemongrass

Lesson 42
SKIN-ENHANCING JUICE

Ingredients

200g curly kale
200g red bell pepper
1 apple
1 piece of ginger

part 9

SMOOTHIES

Background Fruit Class	Banana, avocado, mango, pineapple, dragon fruit, papaya, watermelon, cantaloupe, mangosteen, jackfruit, durian...	Selecting sweet fruits facilitates easy pairing with vegetables.
Vegetable Class	Spinach, rainbow chard, kale, beetroots, pumpkin, zuchinni, brocoli, carrot, bell pepper...	Let's start our smoothie adventure with spinach and kale, which have a subtle, neutral taste. You might find that their presence in the smoothie is hardly noticeable. Next, we can venture into using beetroots and zucchinis, before gradually introducing stronger flavors such as broccoli, carrots, and bell peppers. It's important to start with small quantities of these vegetables. This approach will help our taste buds gradually become accustomed to the unique taste of green vegetables in our smoothies.
Flavor Class	Ingredients: Vanilla essence, young coconut pulp, cocoa powder, cinnamon powder, nutmeg powder, cardamon powder Herbs: Mint, peppermint, cilantro, basil, thyme, ginger, lemon/lime zest. Sweetening: date	Boost the aroma and elevate the appeal of your smoothie.
Nutrient-Enriched Class	Chia Seeds Flaxseeds Hemp Seeds Plant Protein Powder (vanilla or unflavored) Nuts and Seeds	
Liquid Component	Coconut Water Plant-based milk Optionally replace with filtered water + seed/nut butter.	

Lesson 43: MANGO LEMON SMOOTHIE

Ingredients: 2 servings

70g mango

50g coconut flesh (or 2 tablespoons coconut milk from lesson 24)

200ml water

10 macadamia nuts

5 dates

Zest of 1/2 a lemon (or 3 drops lemon essential oil)

1-2 sprigs of peppermint, leaves only (or 2 drops mint essential oil)

50g zucchini (can be replaced with other vegetables like broccoli, spinach)

1/2 teaspoon vanilla extract

Instructions

Blend all ingredients until smooth using a blender.

Lesson 44

CHOCOLATE BANANA SMOOTHIE

Ingredients: 2 servings

200ml filtered water or plant-based milk

20g cashews, soaked for 1-2 hours

1 banana

1 tablespoon sweetener (or 5 dates)

1 tablespoon cocoa powder

2 handfuls of spinach

1/2 teaspoon cinnamon powder

1/2 teaspoon vanilla extract

Instructions

Blend all ingredients until smooth using a blender.

Lesson 45

DRAGON FRUIT AND BEETROOT SMOOTHIE

Ingredients: 2 servings

80g red dragon fruit
80g beetroot
200ml filtered water
1 tablespoon nut butter
1 tablespoon sweetener
(or 5 dates)
3 drops mint essential oil (or fresh mint leaves)

Instructions

Blend all ingredients in a blender until smooth.

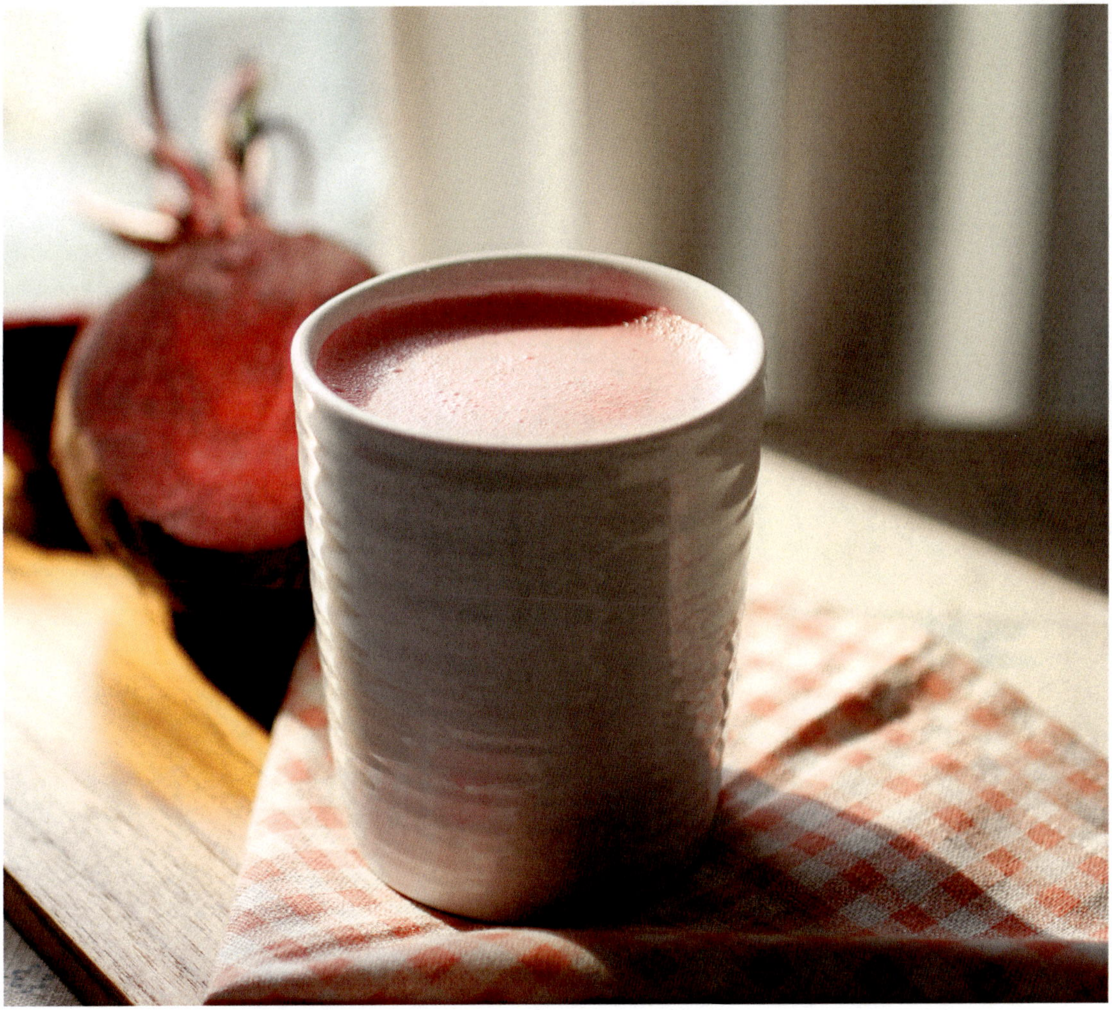

part
10

TECHNIQUES FOR PROCESSING ROLL DISHES

1. Roll Shell
Lettuce
Nori seaweed
Leafly greens
Rice paper (not raw vegan)

2. Sauce
Miso
Nut butter
Raw vegan cheese

3. Fruits
Avocado
Mango
Apple/pear

4. Vegetables
Bell pepper
Cucumber
Tomato
Zucchini
Bean sprouts

Additional Ingredients
White sesame seeds
Almonds
Walnuts
Macadamia nuts

Lesson 46: SUSHI MAKI

Ingredients: 4 servings

300g pickled vegetables: jicamas and carrots (see lesson 23)

Pickled radishes (see lesson 23), optional

1 large avocado (approximately 600g), halved and sliced

2 cups shredded purple cabbage

2 cucumbers, julienned

1 handful of soaked irish moss

1 cup vegan cheese (recipe in lesson 21), or adjust the amount of miso paste for less saltiness

4-5 large sheets of nori seaweed

Instructions

- If available, place a bamboo mat and put a sheet of nori seaweed on top, rough side facing up.

- Spread a tablespoon of vegan cheese on the nori sheet, arrange avocado, pickled jicama and carrots, cucumber, purple cabbage, and soaked irish moss.

- Roll tightly from one end to the other.

- Use a serrated knife or a very sharp knife to cut into bite-sized pieces.

- Serve with tamari sauce if desired.

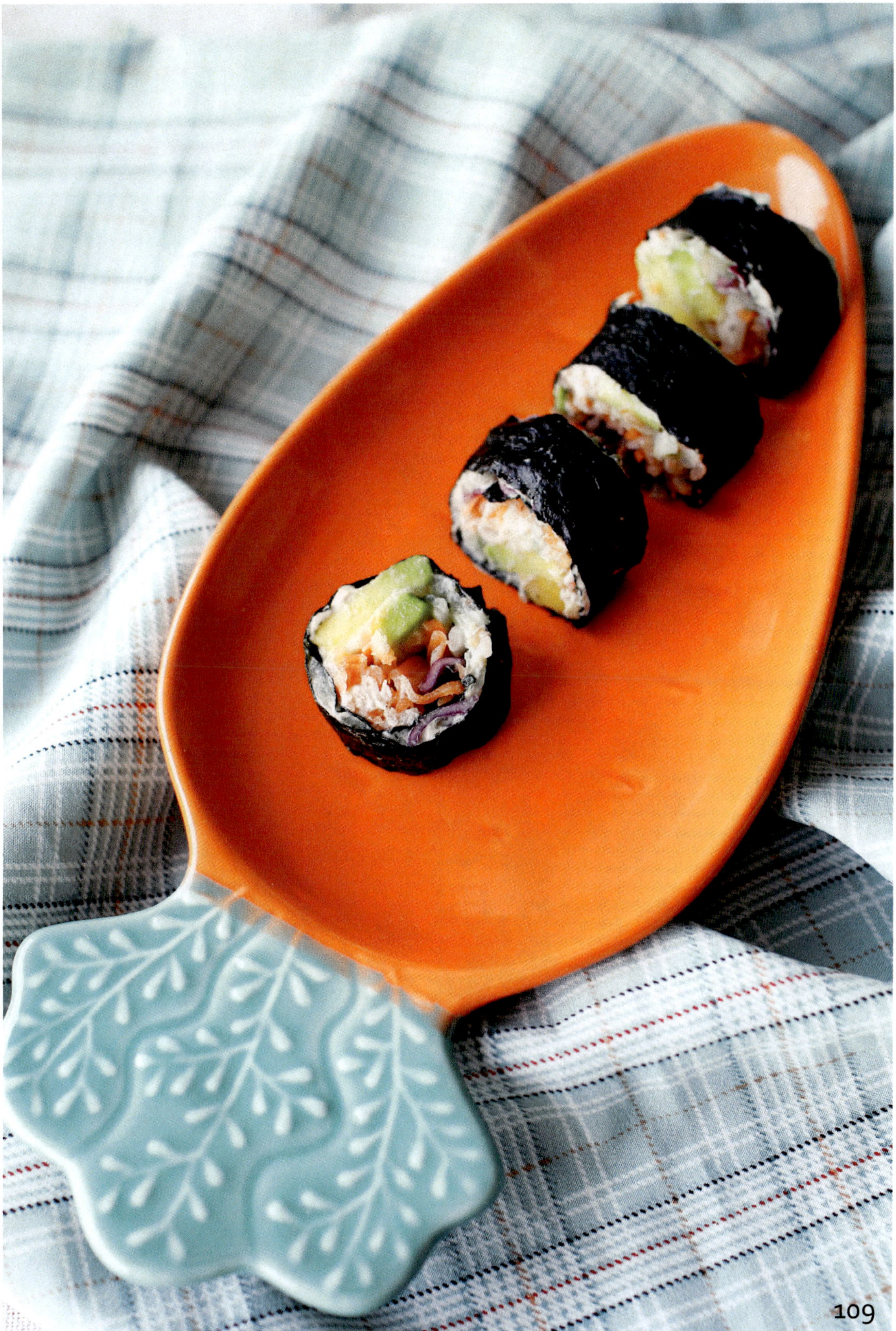

Lesson 47: APPLE TORTILLA

Ingredients: 3-4 servings

Wrapper
2 apples
1 tablespoon coconut oil
2 tablespoons coconut blossom nectar
1 teaspoon cinnamon powder
1/2 teaspoon ginger powder
1/2 teaspoon nutmeg powder

Filling
1-2 tablespoons nut butter (from recipe 25)
1/4 cup macadamia nuts (replaceable with almonds), chopped
10 dates
1/2 cup water (for soaking dates)
2 tablespoons raisins

Instructions

For the Wrapper

- Mix spices in a bowl.
- Slice apples into 0.5cm thick pieces, coat with spices, and dehydrate for 1-2 hours until pliable.

Filling

- Soak dates in 1/2 cup water.
- Blend soaked dates, using the soaked water. Mix with raisins and chopped macadamia nuts.

Assembly

- Wrap the filling mixture between apple slices and fold in half.
- Store in a cool place.
- Enjoy your delicious apple tortilla!

111

Lesson 48 — KOHLRABI DUMPLINGS

Ingredients

Wrapper

1 kohlrabi, thinly sliced
2 tablespoons sesame oil
1 tablespoon lemon juice
1 tablespoon sugar
1 pinch of salt
1 pinch of pepper

Filling

30g carrots, finely chopped
30g cucumber, finely chopped
1/4 cup almond flour
100g avocado (1/2 medium-sized), finely chopped
20g almonds, chopped
2 sprigs of chives, finely chopped
1 handful of cilantro, finely chopped
1/4 teaspoon ginger powder
1/4 teaspoon garlic powder
1/4 teaspoon onion powder
1 teaspoon sugar
1 teaspoon tamari

Decoration

1 handful of chives for tying dumplings (optional)

Instructions

Wrapper

- Slice or peel the kohlrabi into thin, round slices.
- Prepare a spice mixture by combining sesame oil, lemon juice, sugar, salt, and pepper.
- Soak the kohlrabi slices in the spice mixture for at least 10 minutes to soften.

Filling

- In a mixing bowl, combine all the filling ingredients, excluding the avocado.
- Add the finely chopped avocado last to prevent it from becoming mushy.

Assembly

- Take one of the softened kohlrabi slices.
- Place a portion of the prepared filling in the center of the kohlrabi slice.
- Roll the kohlrabi slice to enclose the filling.
- If desired, secure the dumpling with a chive tie.
- Enjoy your homemade Kohlrabi Dumplings!

113

Lesson 49

BEETROOT RAVIOLI

Ingredients: 2 servings

Wrapper

1 small beetroot
2 tablespoons olive oil (or sesame oil)
1 tablespoon vinegar
1 tablespoon sugar
1 pinch of salt
1 pinch of pepper

Filling

1/2 cup pumpkin seeds
1 teaspoon onion powder
1 teaspoon garlic powder
2 tablespoons nutritional yeast
2 tablespoons olive oil (or sesame oil)
2 tablespoons water
1 pinch of pepper
1 pinch of salt

Instructions

Wrapper

- Slice or shave the beetroot into thin, round slices.
- Prepare a spice mixture by combining olive oil, vinegar, sugar, salt, and pepper.
- Soak the beetroot slices in the spice mixture for at least 10 minutes to soften. You can refrigerate them overnight for better flavor absorption.

For the Filling

- In a blender, combine pumpkin seeds, onion powder, garlic powder, nutritional yeast, olive oil (or sesame oil), water, pepper, and salt.
- Blend all the filling ingredients until you achieve a smooth consistency.

Assembly

- Take one of the softened beetroot slices.
- Place a portion of the prepared filling in the center of the beetroot slice.
- Fold the beetroot slice in half, creating a semi-circle shape.
- Press around the edges to seal the ravioli, ensuring the filling is enclosed.
- Enjoy your homemade Beetroot ravioli!

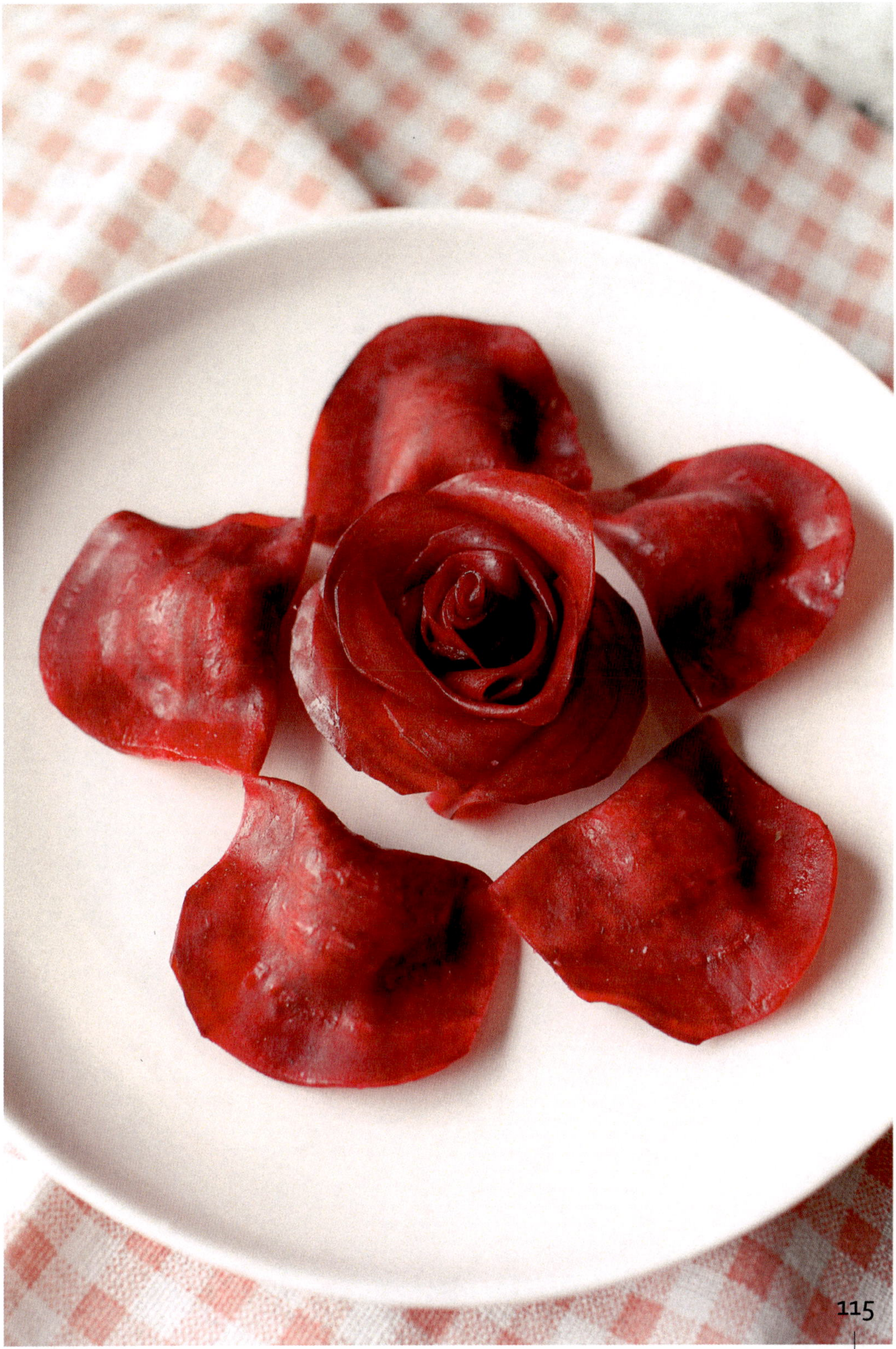

Notes

part 11

TECHNIQUES FOR MAKING RAW NOODLES

1. Vegetable Spiralizer

A spiralizer is a handy tool for turning vegetables into noodle-like shapes. It works well with vegetables like zucchini, carrots, and cucumbers. Choose a spiralizer with various blade options to create different noodle sizes.

2. Julienne Peeler

If you don't have a spiralizer, a julienne peeler can be a great alternative. It shreds vegetables into thin, noodle-like strips. It's perfect for making carrot and cucumber noodles.

3. Mandoline Slicer

A mandoline slicer with a julienne attachment can also be used to create uniform vegetable noodles. Adjust the thickness of the julienne setting to your preference.

4. Knife Skills

If you're comfortable with a knife, you can hand-cut vegetable noodles. Slice vegetables into thin strips, and then stack and cut them into narrower strips to mimic the shape

Lesson 50

"ZUCCHINI" WITH PESTO SAUCE

Ingredients: 2 servings

For the noodles
1 zucchini
100g cherry tomatoes
1/4 cup chopped walnuts

For the Sauce
1/2 cup soaked cashews
1 cup water
1 tablespoon nutritional yeast
1 tablespoon maple syrup (or other sweetener)
1 tablespoon sesame oil
1/2 tablespoon lemon juice or apple cider vinegar
1/2 teaspoon garlic powder
1/2 teaspoon onion powder
1 tablespoon dried basil or 50g fresh basil
1 pinch of salt

Instructions

For the Noodles
- Use a spiralizer to transform the zucchini into long, noodle-like strands. If you don't have a spiralizer, a julienne peeler can be used to achieve a similar effect.
- Combine the zucchini strands with cherry tomatoes and chopped walnuts in a mixing bowl.

For the Sauce
- Blend all the ingredients for the sauce until they reach a smooth consistency.

To Serve
- Arrange the zucchini noodles, cherry tomatoes, and walnuts on a plate.
- Generously drizzle the prepared sauce over the noodles.
- Sprinkle additional chopped walnuts over the top for added crunch and flavor.
- Garnish with fresh basil leaves to enhance the presentation and taste.

Lesson 51
PAD THAI (THAI-STYLE CUCUMBER NOODLES)

Ingredients: 2 servings

2 cucumbers
1/4 bell pepper, sliced into strips
1/4 cup cherry tomatoes, halved
1 bunch of chives, finely chopped (can be substituted with green onions)
1 handful of cilantro, finely chopped
1 handful of mint leaves, finely chopped

Sauce

1/2 cup water
1 tablespoon nut butter (peanut, almond, or preferred type)
2 tablespoons vegan fish sauce (or soy sauce/tamari as an alternative)
2 tablespoons tamarind juice
1/2 teaspoon ginger powder
1/2 teaspoon garlic powder
1/2 teaspoon onion powder
1 tablespoon sesame oil
1/4 teaspoon salt
1 tablespoon sweetener (adjust to taste, e.g., brown sugar, maple syrup, or agave nectar)

Instructions

Noodles

- If you have a spiralizer, spiralize the cucumbers into long, noodle-like strands. If not, you can use a julienne peeler to create long strands.
- Mix the cucumber noodles with cherry tomatoes and sliced bell pepper.

Sauce

- In a bowl, whisk together all the sauce ingredients: water, nut butter, vegan fish sauce (or alternative), tamarind juice, ginger powder, garlic powder, onion powder, sesame oil, salt, and sweetener. Adjust the sweetener to your preferred level of sweetness.

Assembly

- In a large mixing bowl, combine the cucumber noodles, cherry tomatoes, sliced bell pepper, finely chopped chives (or green onions), cilantro, and mint leaves.
- Drizzle the prepared sauce over the mixed ingredients in the bowl.
- Toss everything together until the sauce coats the noodles and vegetables evenly.

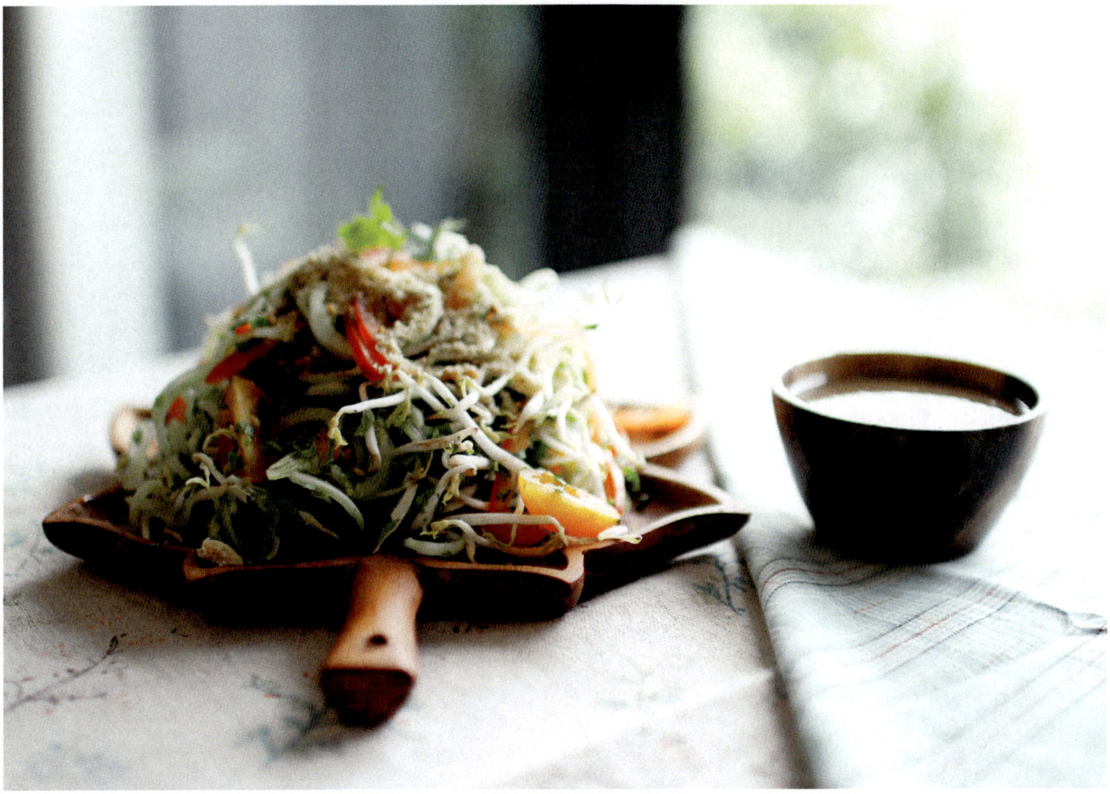

Lesson 52: VIETNAMESE "BUN"

Ingredients

100g young coconut, shredded for the "noodles" part
30g lettuce, finely chopped
30g bean sprouts
30g cucumber, julienned
30g elsholtzia/perilla leaves, shredded
30g nuts, chopped

Sauce
1 teaspoon ginger powder
1 teaspoon lemongrass powder
1 cinnamon stick
1 teaspoon dried tangerine peel (Citrus Reticulata peel)
1 tablespoon tamari sauce
1 tablespoon sugar
Pulp of 1/2 passion fruit (with seeds)
1 tablespoon tahini (refer to lesson 25)
1 tablespoon water

Optional Garnishes
Chopped cilantro
Roasted sesame seeds

Instructions

Preparing the Sauce

- Soak the cinnamon stick and dried tangerine peel in tamari sauce for at least 15 minutes or overnight. Remove the cinnamon stick and dried orange peel, using only the tamari liquid.

- In a separate bowl, mix the sauce ingredients: ginger powder, lemongrass powder, tamari-soaked liquid, sugar, passion fruit pulp (with seeds), sesame butter, and water. Stir the ingredients well to create the sauce.

Assembly

- In a large bowl, combine the shredded young coconut (used as noodles), finely chopped lettuce, bean sprouts, julienned cucumber, shredded elsholtzia/perilla leaves, and chopped dried seeds.

- When serving, drizzle the prepared sauce over the mixed ingredients in the bowl.

- Optionally, garnish the dish with chopped cilantro, roasted sesame seeds, or crushed peanuts for added flavor and texture.

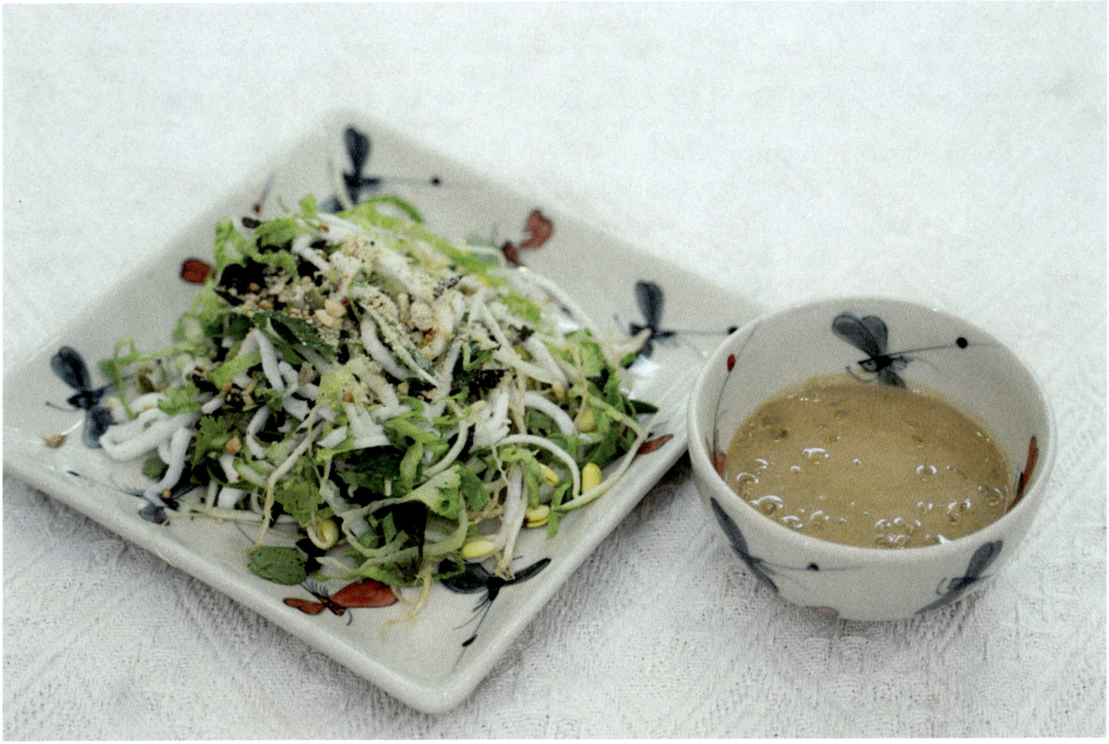

Lesson 53

MAC N CHEESE

Ingredients: 2 servings

2 cups young coconut meat, cut into small pieces resembling macaroni noodles

Sauce
1 cup cashews
2 tablespoons nutritional yeast
1 teaspoon paprika powder
1/4 teaspoon turmeric powder
1/2 teaspoon garlic powder
1/2 teaspoon onion powder
1/2 teaspoon salt
1 cup water
2 Medjool dates (adjust sweetness according to preference)

Instructions

- Begin by preparing the "macaroni" by cutting the young coconut meat into small pieces resembling macaroni noodles.

- In a blender, combine the sauce ingredients: cashews, nutritional yeast, paprika powder, turmeric powder, garlic powder, onion powder, salt, water, and Medjool dates. Blend until the mixture becomes smooth and creamy. Adjust the sweetness by adding more dates if desired.

- Pour the creamy sauce over the prepared "macaroni" and mix well to ensure that the "macaroni" is coated evenly.

part 12

PORRIDGE AND SOUP PROCESSING TECHNIQUE

Lesson 54 — CARROT SOUP

Ingredients: 2 servings

1 carrot
1.5 cups water
1/2 cup cashews
3 dates
1 small piece of coconut flesh (about 30g)
1 small piece of ginger, finely chopped
1 lemongrass stalk, white part only, finely chopped
1 tablespoon tamari
1/2 teaspoon garlic powder
1/2 teaspoon onion powder
1/4 teaspoon salt
1 pinch of pepper
Fresh cilantro for garnish

Instructions

- Blend all ingredients until smooth, excluding cilantro.
- Can strain through a fine mesh sieve for a smoother consistency (as lemongrass may still have fibers).

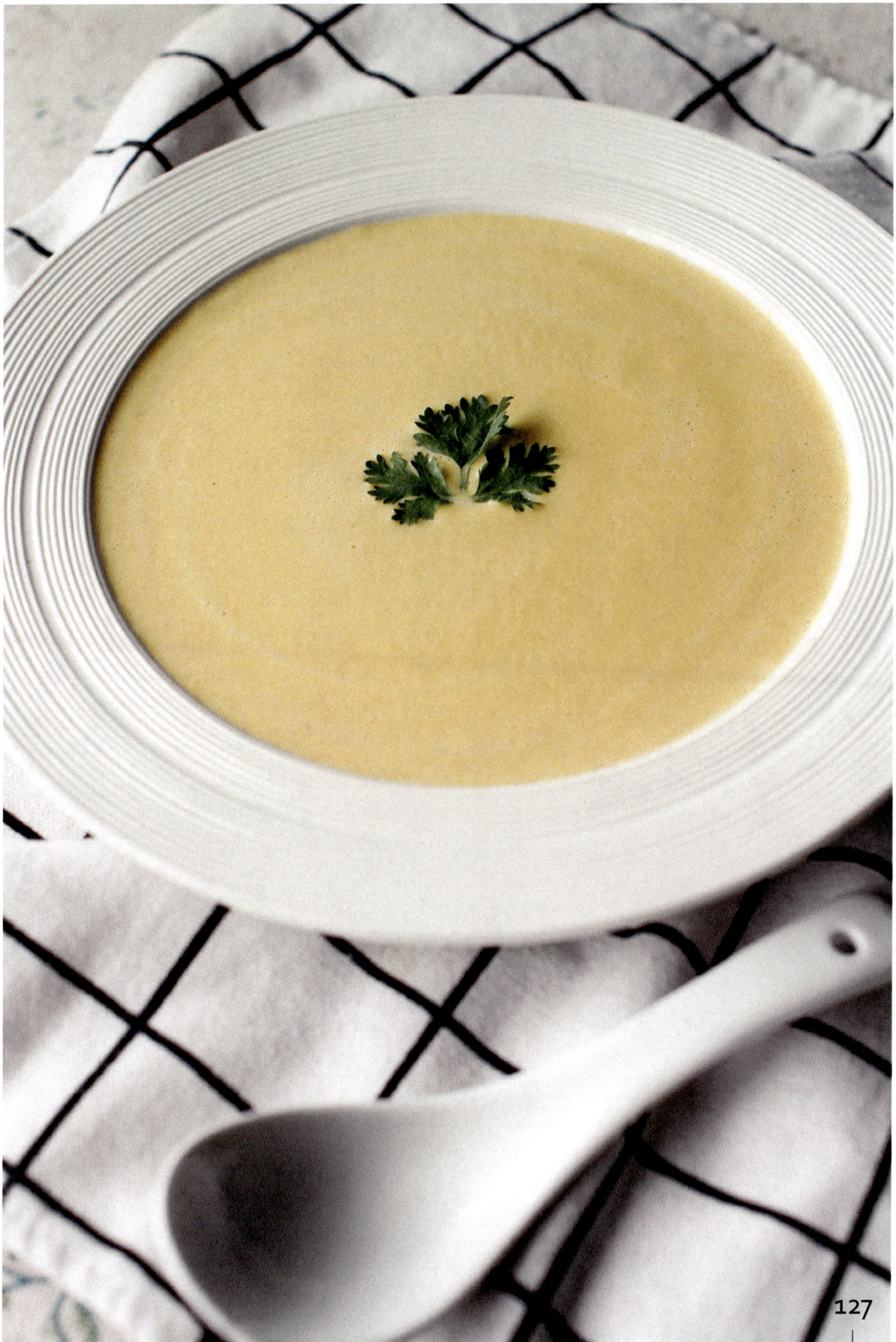

Lesson 55: TOMATO SOUP

Ingredients: 2 servings

380g ripe tomatoes (about 5 Roma tomatoes)

1/4 cup almonds, soaked for 6-8 hours

1 cup water

5 dates (adjust according to tomato sweetness)

2 tablespoons nutritional yeast

1 teaspoon dried basil

1/2 teaspoon dried rosemary

1 teaspoon cinnamon powder

1 teaspoon garlic powder

1 teaspoon green onion powder

1/4 teaspoon black pepper

1 pinch of salt

Instructions

- In a food processor or blender, combine the chopped tomatoes, soaked almonds, water, dates, nutritional yeast, dried basil, dried rosemary, cinnamon powder, garlic powder, green onion powder, black pepper, and a pinch of salt.

- Blend until the mixture is smooth and creamy.

- Taste the soup and adjust the sweetness by adding more dates if needed.

- Serve the tomato soup hot, garnished with fresh basil leaves or your preferred toppings.

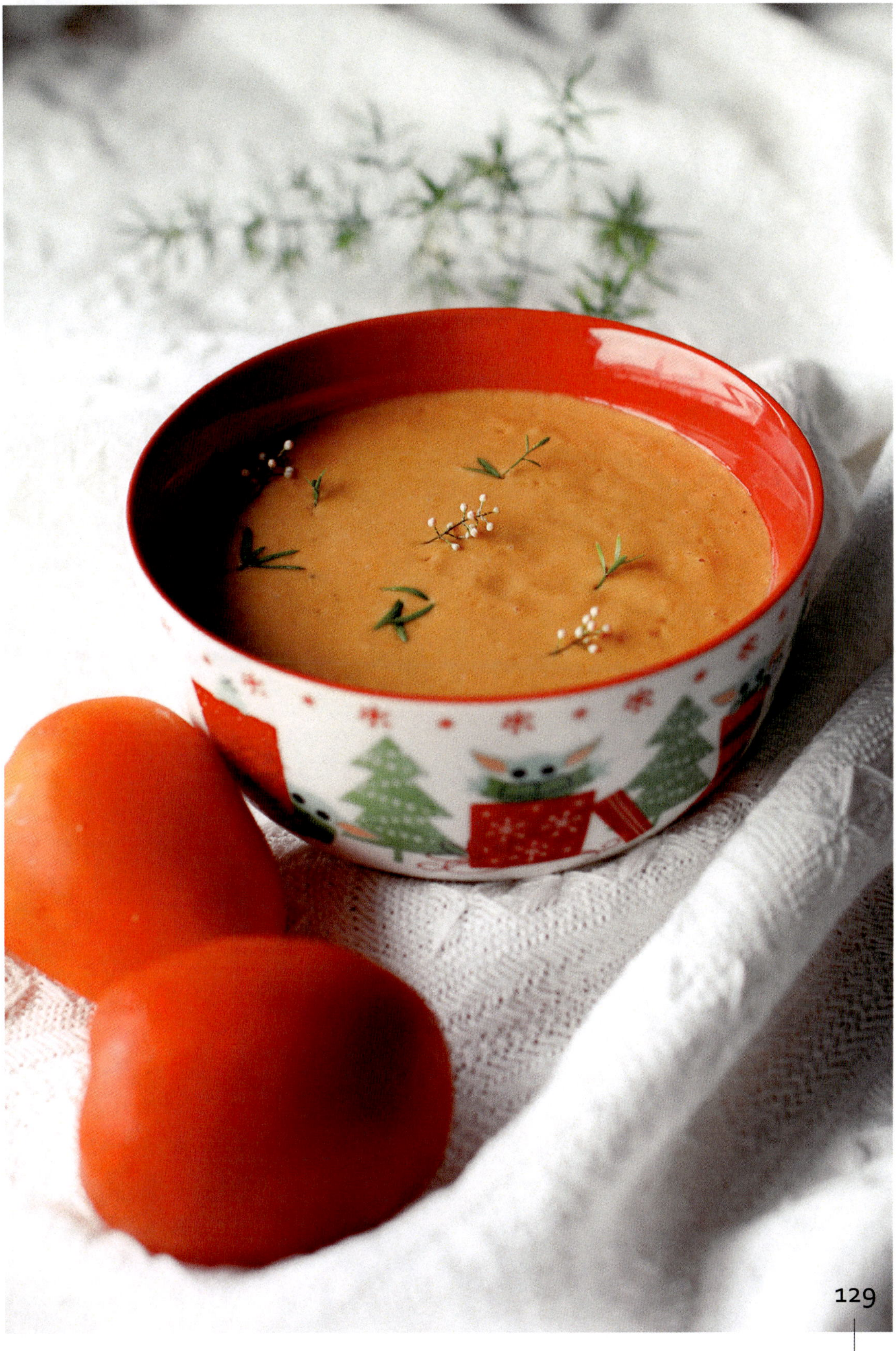

Lesson 56: PUMPKIN CURRY SOUP

Ingredients: 2 servings

300g red pumpkin, peeled and diced
1 cup water
1/2 cup pumpkin seeds
40g fresh coconut flesh, grated
1 tablespoon curry powder
1/4 teaspoon salt
1/4 teaspoon turmeric
1/4 teaspoon onion powder
1/4 teaspoon garlic powder
1/4 teaspoon nutmeg
1/4 teaspoon ginger powder
1 pinch of pepper
1 tablespoon coconut sugar (optional, depending on the sweetness of the pumpkin)

Garnish
2 tablespoons pumpkin seeds (or other preferred garnishes)

Instructions

- In a food processor or blender, combine all the ingredients.
- Blend until smooth.
- If desired, sprinkle pumpkin seeds or other preferred garnishes on top before serving.

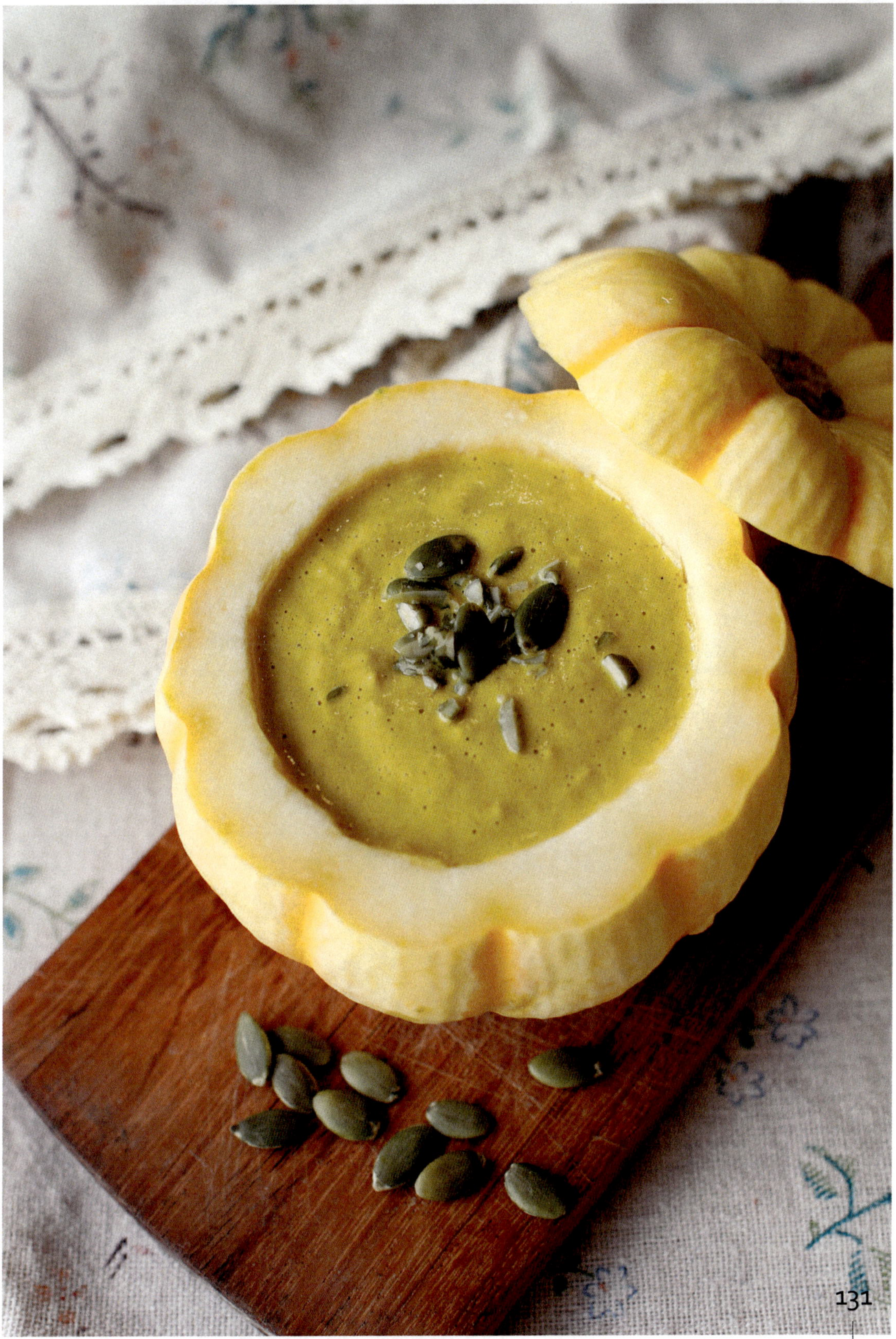

Lesson 57

AVOCADO PORRIDGE

Ingredients: 2 servings

2 cups blended jicama and carrot juice (500g jicama, 120g carrot)

1 cup water

1/2 cup oats

1/2 cup cashews

200g avocado (1/2 large avocado)

8 dates

4 tablespoons nutritional yeast

1 teaspoon ginger powder

1 teaspoon onion powder

1 teaspoon garlic powder

1 handful of cilantro

1 pinch of salt

1 mint leaves or 2 drops of mint oil

1 pinch of pepper

Instructions

- In a blender or food processor, combine all the ingredients.

- Blend until smooth.

- Serve in bowls and garnish with your choice of toppings, such as sliced avocado, chopped nuts, or fresh herbs.

- Optional Toppings: Feel free to customize your porridge with additional toppings for added flavor and texture

SALAD PROCESSING TECHNIQUES

Ingredients for making salads

Leafy vegetables	Lecttuce Glass lecttuce Romaine lecttuce Iceberg lecttuce (American cabbage) Kale
Sturdy Vegetables	Cucumber Zucchini Bell pepper Carrot Beetroot Kohlrabi Red radish
Fresh fruits	Cherry tomatoes Apple Avocado Green/ripe mango Grape fruit Orange Green papaya Strawberry Grapes Young mangosteen Pomegranate Peach
Dried fruits	Dried apricots Raisins Cranberries Goji berries Dates
Dried seeds	Almond Walnuts Pumpkin seeds Sunflower seeds
Herbs	Coriander Elsholtzia Polygonum Peppermint Sawleaf
Other ingredients	Green/black olives Onions (can be pickled)

Lesson 58: RUSSIAN SALAD

Ingredients: 2 servings

100g carrots, diced

30g pickled onions, diced (from recipe 23)

200g cucumber, diced

200g avocado, diced

100g aloe vera, washed and diced

200g jicama, diced

50g irish moss, soaked and wash thorougly, finely chopped

50g macadamia nuts, finely chopped

MAYONNAISE SAUCE:

1 cup cashews, soaked

1 tablespoon lemon juice/apple cider vinegar

1/2 teaspoon garlic powder

1/2 teaspoon onion powder

1/4 cup coconut flesh

1/2 cup water (or replace coconut and water with 120g raw coconut cream)

1 tablespoon olive oil

1 teaspoon yellow mustard powder

1/4 teaspoon salt

Instructions

- Blend the sauce ingredients until smooth.

- Mix all ingredients, excluding avocado and sauce.

- Gently fold in the avocado and drizzle with the sauce. Serve and enjoy.

Lesson 59: MINT APRICOT ORANGE SALAD

Ingredients: 2 servings

Salad Ingredients
100g lettuce
30g rocket arugula (optional)
50g zucchini
30g purple cabbage
30g bell pepper
1 orange, segmented
5 dried apricots (or substitute with raisins)
10 walnuts
30g peas
1 tablespoon white sesame seeds (for sprinkling)

Mint Apricot Mango Dressing
1 tablespoon white sesame seeds
1/4 cup sesame oil
2 oranges (400g), juiced
4 dried apricots
1/2 cup peppermint leaves
1/4 teaspoon salt
1/2 teaspoon onion powder
1 pinch of pepper

Instructions

- Blend the dressing ingredients until smooth.
- Mix the dressing with the salad ingredients before serving.

Note: If not consumed immediately after preparation, store the salad and dressing separately in the refrigerator to prevent the salad from becoming watery.

Enjoy your Mint Apricot Orange Salad!

137

MIXED SPINACH SALAD WITH COCONUT AVOCADO DRESSING

Lesson 60

Ingredients: 2 servings

Salad
100g spinach
100g beetroot, shredded
2 red radishes, thinly sliced
2 tablespoons raisins
10 macadamia nuts, chopped
Lime leaves, thinly sliced

Dressing
30g avocado
7g coriander
6 dates
1 tablespoon apple cider vinegar
1/2 teaspoon ginger powder
1/2 teaspoon garlic powder
1 cup water
50g young coconut flesh
1 pinch of black pepper

Instructions

- Blend dressing ingredients until smooth.
- Mix the dressing with the vegetables when serving.

Note: Store the salad and dressing separately in the refrigerator if not consumed immediately after preparation. This is important because a pre-mixed salad tends to release water, affecting its texture and freshness.

Enjoy your mixed spinach salad with coconut avocado dressing!

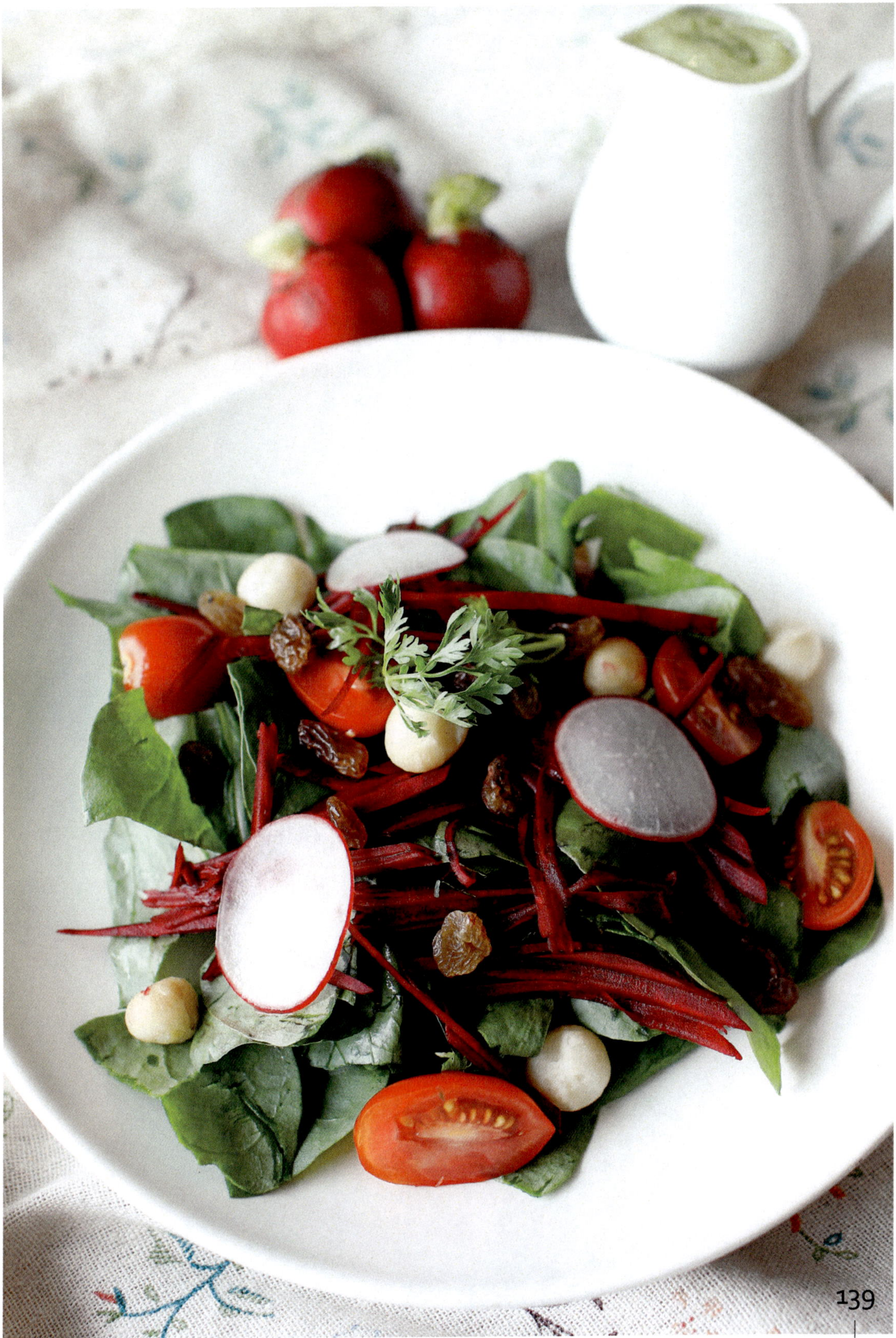

Lesson 61: KALE SALAD WITH CASHEW

Ingredients: 2 servings

50g curly kale, stems removed (massaged with 1 tbsp olive oil and 1/2 tbsp lemon juice)
30g broccoli, finely chopped
50g yellow bell pepper, thinly sliced
50g cherry tomatoes (approximately 5), halved
30g carrots, julienned
50g apple, julienned
50g avocado, sliced
5 black olives, sliced in half
2 tablespoons dried cranberries
2 tablespoons chopped almonds

Dressing
1/2 cup soaked cashews
2 dates
1/2 cup water
1/2 tablespoon tamari sauce
2 tablespoons kumquat juice
1 tablespoon nutritional yeast
2 tablespoons olive oil
1 teaspoon garlic powder
1 teaspoon onion powder
A pinch of pepper
A pinch of salt

Instructions

- Massage kale with olive oil and kumquat juice (or vinegar) until tender.

- Blend all dressing ingredients, except salt, until smooth. Add salt to taste.

- Pour the sauce over the salad ingredients and toss everything together until the sauce coats the ingredients evenly.

- Texture: Refreshing and crunchy

- Storage: You can refrigerate the salad for freshness, but it's best enjoyed fresh.

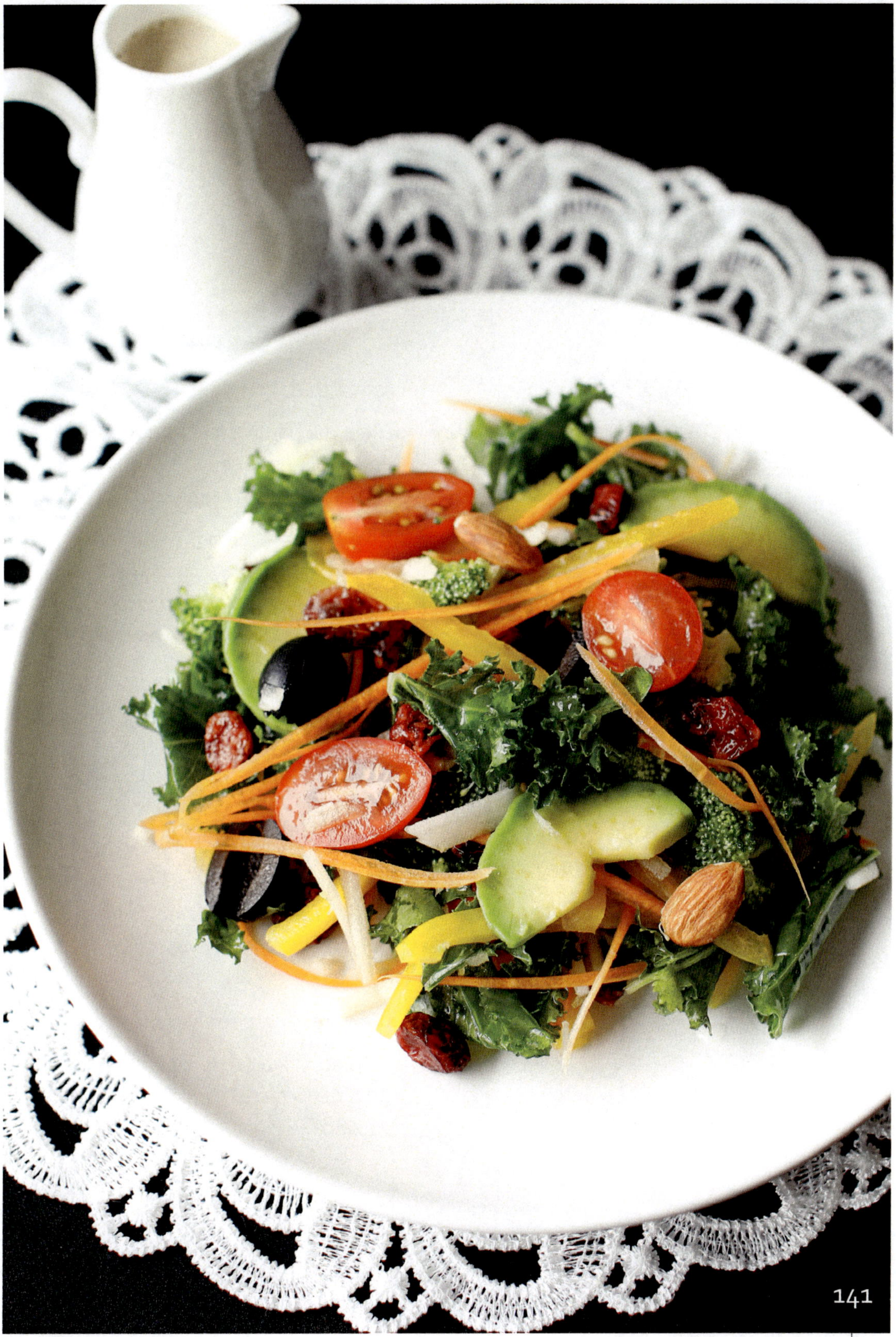

Lesson 62

GREEN PAPAYA SALAD WITH TAMARIND SAUCE

Ingredients: 3-4 servings

500g green papaya (approximately 1 medium-sized papaya)

50g carrot, julienned

1 green mango, julienned (or substitute with papaya)

100g cherry tomatoes, halved or quartered

50g pumpkin seeds, finely chopped (or substitute with other seeds)

1 chili pepper, thinly sliced (for spice)

Sauce

30g tamarind pulp (from 2 tamarind fruits or tamarind concentrate)

12g vegan fish sauce

40g sugar

2.5g salt

1 tablespoon galangal root powder

Instructions

- Peel the papaya and remove the seeds. Julienne the papaya and soak it in salted water, then drain.

- In a large mixing bowl, combine the julienned papaya, julienned carrot, Thailand mango (or papaya), cherry tomatoes, and sliced chili pepper.

- In a separate bowl, prepare the sauce. Mix the tamarind pulp (or tamarind concentrate), vegan fish sauce, sugar, salt, and galangal root powder until well combined.

- Pour the sauce over the salad ingredients and toss everything together until the sauce coats the ingredients evenly.

- Texture: Crunchy and refreshing

- Storage: You can refrigerate the salad for freshness, but it's best enjoyed fresh.

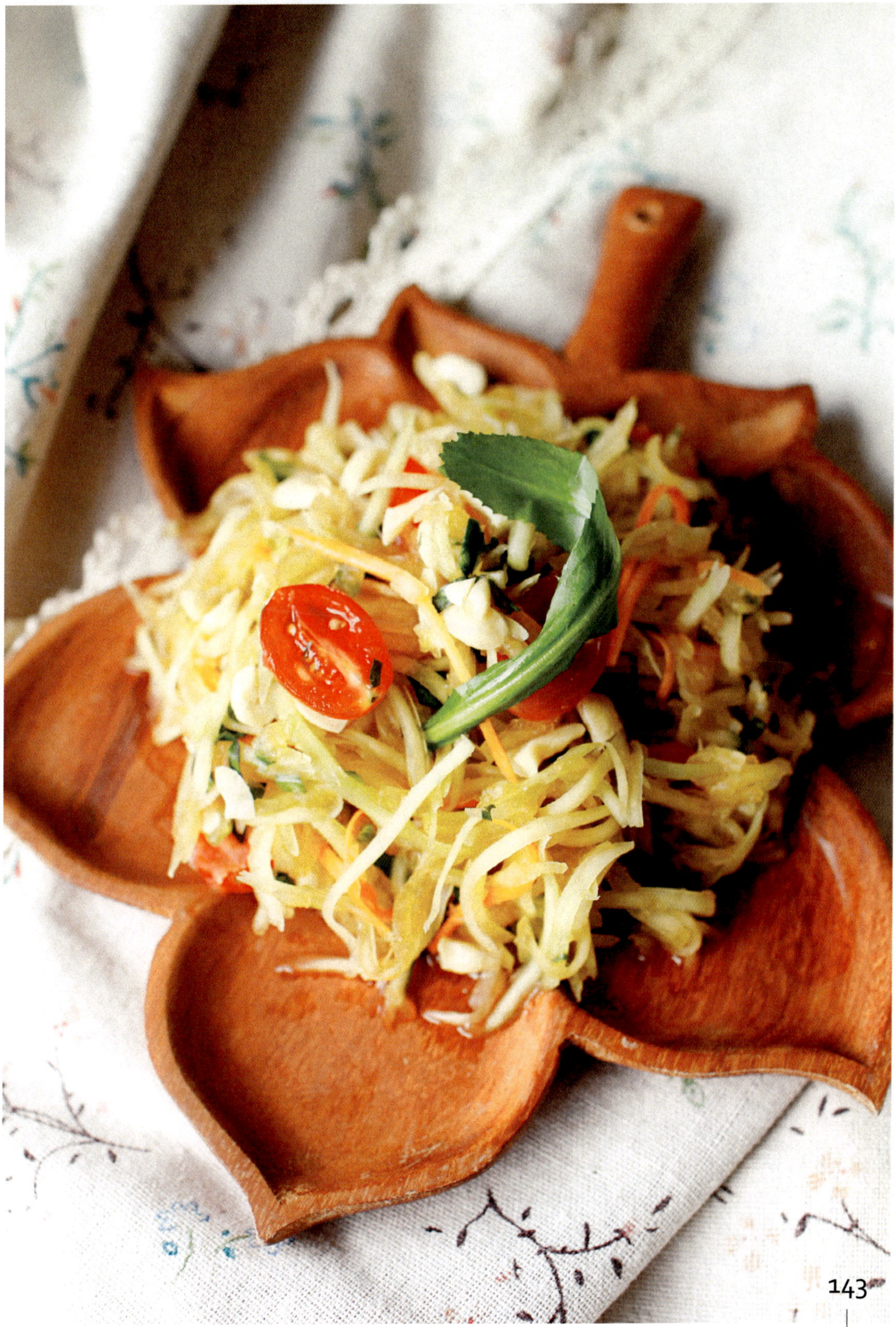

Lesson 63: BANANA FLOWER SALAD

Ingredients: 3-4 servings

1 banana flower
50g zucchini, julienned
50g almonds, finely chopped
20g white sesame seeds
50g purple cabbage, julienned
Fresh herbs: coriander, peppermint, elsholtzia

Sauce
40g brown sugar
2.5g salt
20g apple cider vinegar
12g vegan fish sauce

Instructions

- Preparing the Banana Flower:
- Begin by peeling away the tough outer layers of the banana flower.
- Once the outer layers are removed, thinly slice the banana flower.
- In a bowl, prepare a mixture of 1 tablespoon of vinegar and 1 tablespoon of salt.
- Soak the sliced banana flower in this mixture for approximately 15 minutes. This step helps to prevent the banana flower from discoloring.
- After soaking, drain the banana flower well, ensuring all excess liquid is removed.

Making the Dipping Sauce:

- In a separate bowl, combine all the ingredients for the dipping sauce. Stir them together until well mixed.
- Add the purple cabbage to the sauce last. This is to prevent the color from the cabbage bleeding into the sauce and altering its appearance.
- Texture: Crunchy and refreshing
- Storage: You can refrigerate the salad for freshness, but it's best enjoyed fresh.

145

Lesson 64: POMELO SALAD

Ingredients: 2 servings

1 small pomelo
50g shredded carrots
50g shredded cucumber
50g small shredded young coconut
Zest of 1 lemon
1/4 cup walnuts (replaceable with other nuts)
10g finely chopped Polygonum
10g sesame seeds

Dressing
40g brown sugar
2.5g salt
20g lemon juice
12g tamari

Instructions

Prepare the Pomelo

- Begin by peeling the pomelo. Once peeled, gently separate the segments.

Dressing Preparation

- Take the ingredients for the dressing and mixed well. Ensure that they are thoroughly mixed and fully dissolved.

Combining Ingredients

- In a large mixing bowl, combine the prepared pomelo segments with the other ingredients.

- Finally, add the dressing to the bowl.

- Toss everything together gently, ensuring that the pomelo and other ingredients are evenly coated with the dressing.

- Texture: Refreshing and crunchy

- Storage: You can refrigerate the salad for freshness, but it's best enjoyed fresh.

part 14

PASTRY AND DESSERT MAKING TECHNIQUES

Lesson 65

TRUFFLE PROTEIN

Ingredients: 6-8 servings

1 1/2 cups walnuts, finely chopped

1 cup almond flour (can be substituted with oats)

1 tablespoon pumpkin seeds

1 tablespoon sunflower seeds

2 tablespoons nut butter

10 pitted dates, soaked in 1/4 cup warm water (20-30 minutes)

1 tablespoon chia seeds

2 tablespoons goji berries

1 teaspoon vanilla extract

1-2 teaspoons cocoa powder (optional, for a cocoa flavor)

Instructions

- Process dates, soaking water, and almond flour in a food processor until smooth and creamy.

- Pour the mixture into a bowl, then add all the remaining ingredients.

- Mix well until everything is evenly combined.

- Shape the mixture into bite-sized balls and place them on a tray.

- Store the truffle protein balls in an airtight container in the refrigerator for 5-7 days.

- Storage: Keep the protein balls refrigerated to maintain freshness.

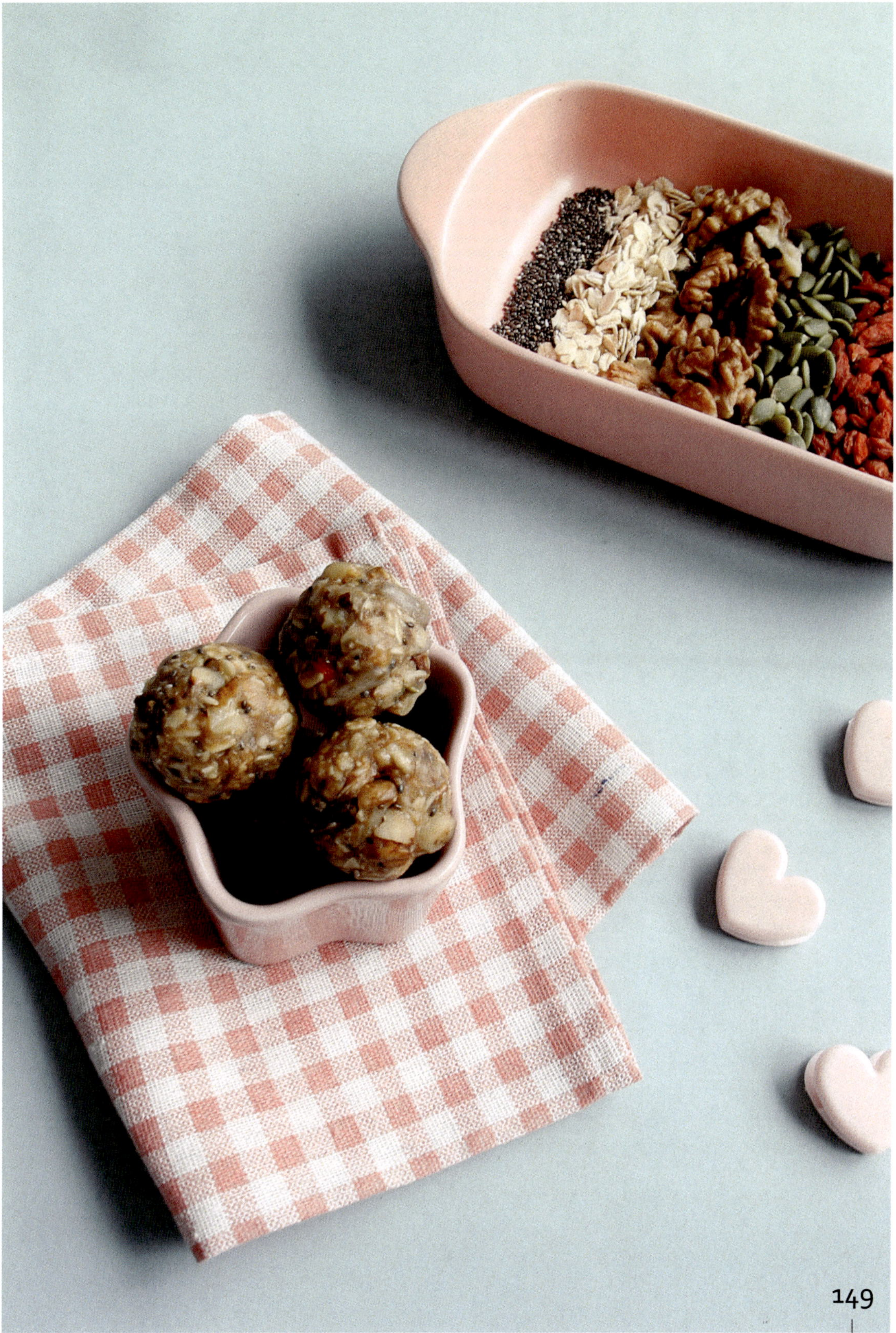

Lesson 66: FRUIT CHEESECAKE

Ingredients: 4 - 6 servings

Cake Crust

3/4 cup almonds
1/4 cup rolled oats
1/4 cup desiccated coconut flakes
6 dates
2 tablespoons coconut oil
1/4 cup water
1 pinch of salt

Cream Filling

2 cups cashews, soaked overnight, drained
10 dates
1/4 cup young coconut meat (or coconut cream)
1/2 cup water
1 banana
6 strawberries (plus 3-4 for decoration)
1 teaspoon vanilla extract (or scraped vanilla bean)
2 tablespoons lemon juice
4 tablespoons coconut oil

Note: Strawberries can be replaced with 100-150g of other fruits such as avocado, mango, blueberries.

Instructions

Cake Crust

- Blend all crust ingredients in a blender until a sticky mixture forms.
- Press the mixture into a cake mold using your hands or the bottom of a cup to create an even crust.

Cream Filling

- Blend all cream filling ingredients in a blender or food processor until smooth.
- Pour the cream filling over the crust in the cake mold.
- Freeze the cheesecake for at least 4 hours before serving.
- For longer freezing times, let it sit outside for 5-10 minutes before enjoying.
- Decorate the cheesecake with sliced strawberries or your choice of fruits before serving.
- Texture: Creamy and smooth
- Storage: Store the cheesecake in the freezer for freshness, and let it sit at room temperature briefly before serving.

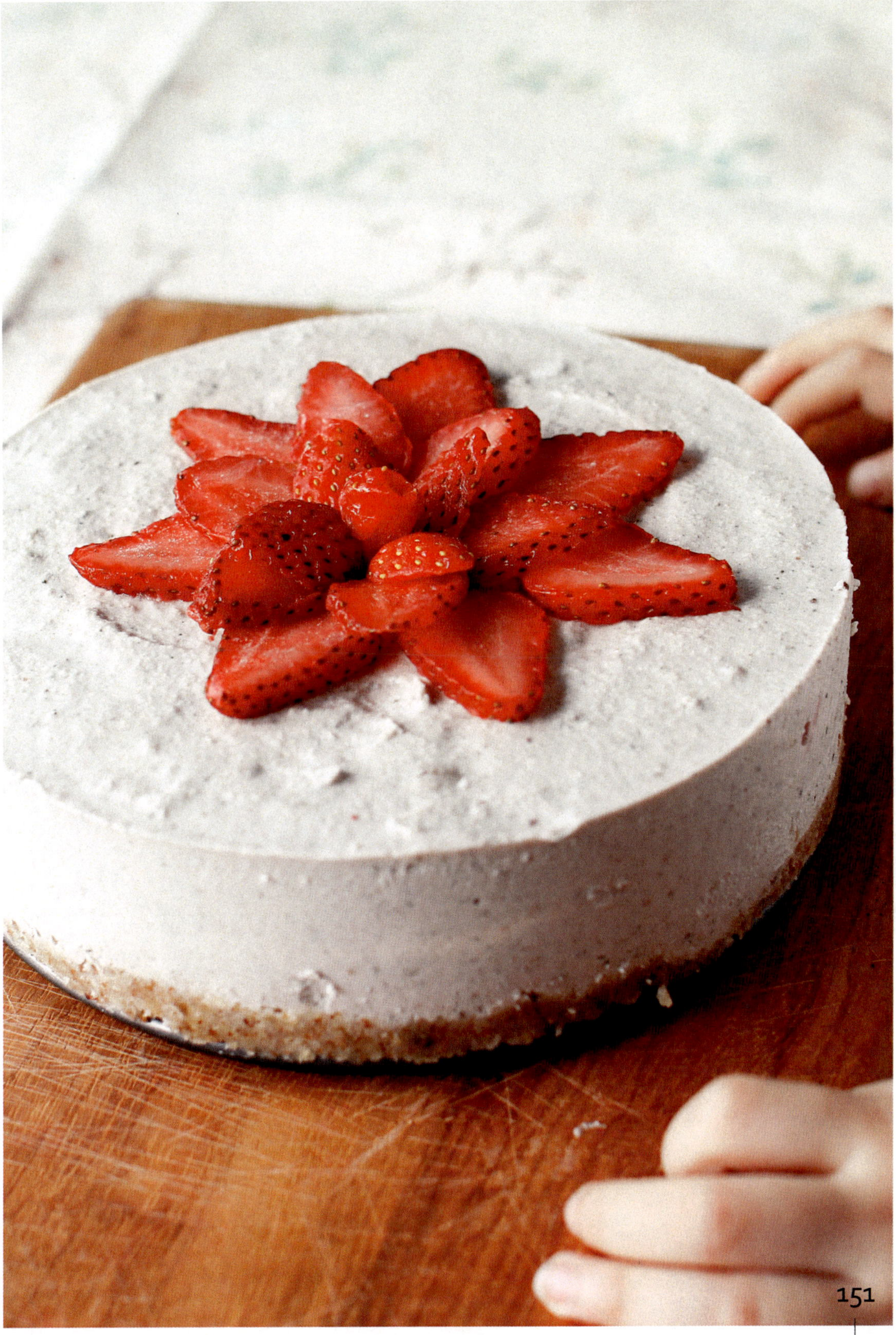

Lesson 67: MANGO MOUSSE

Ingredients: 4-6 servings

Cake crust
2 cups walnuts
10 dates, soaked and drained
1/4 cup coconut oil
Pinch of salt

Mousse filling
1 cup cashews, soaked
1 mango (about 300g), sliced
1 piece of coconut meat (80g)
1/2 cup water
1/2 cup coconut sugar
1/4 cup coconut oil
1/2 tablespoon vanilla extract
2 teaspoons lemon juice
Zest of 1 lemon
1 teaspoon xanthan gum

Decoration
1 fresh mango

Instructions

Cake Crust

- Grind the ingredients in a food processor until sticky.
- Press the mixture into a lined mold with parchment paper.

Mousse Filling

- Blend all ingredients (except xanthan gum) until smooth.
- Add xanthan gum and blend for an additional 30 seconds.
- Pour the mixture into the mold and chill in the fridge for at least 2 hours.

Decoration

- Decorate with fresh mango slices.
- Enjoy your delicious mango mousse!

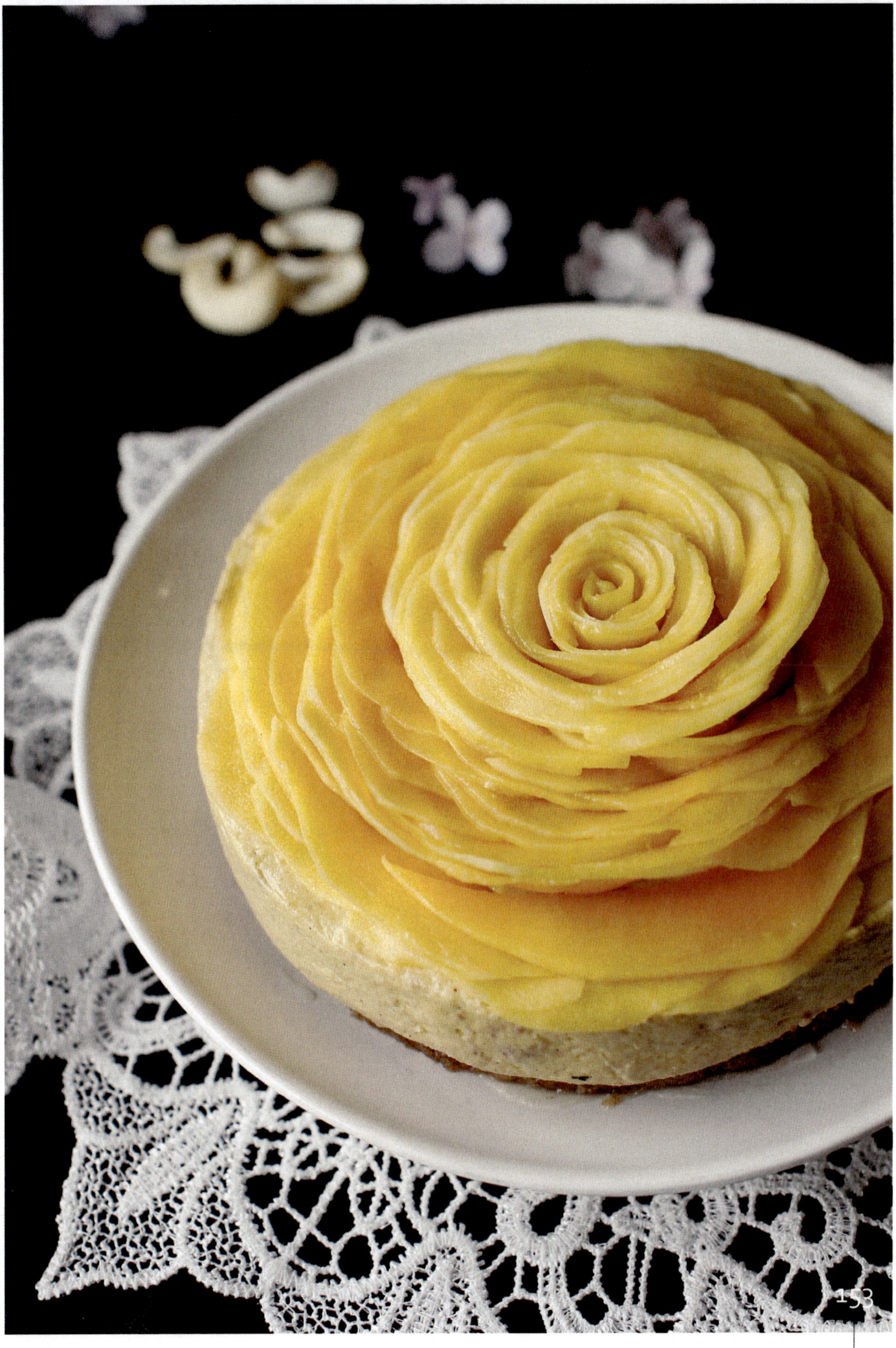

Lesson 68: BROWNIES

Ingredients: 16 small pieces

Brownie Base

1 cup walnuts

1 cup almonds

10 dates soaked in 1/4 cup water (reserve the soaking water)

1/2 cup cocoa powder

1 teaspoon vanilla

1 pinch of salt

Ganache Fillings

1 cup macadamia nuts, soaked

1/2 cup coconut oil

1/4 cup coconut sugar

1/4 cup cocoa powder

1 teaspoon vanilla

1/2 cup water

1/2 cup cranberries

Instructions

Brownie Base

- Place the ingredients in a food processor. Grind until they combine into a sticky mixture.
- Transfer this mixture into a tray or mold lined with parchment paper.
- Use a spatula to evenly smooth out the surface.

Ganache Fillings

- Blend all the ingredients for the ganache, except for the cranberries, until you achieve a smooth consistency.
- Gently fold in the cranberries into the mixture.
- Evenly spread this ganache mixture over the prepared brownie base.

Shaping and Setting

- Place the tray in the fridge and allow to chill for a minimum of 1 hour for the brownie to set.
- Once firmly set, remove from the mold.
- Cut the brownie into small, bite-sized pieces for serving.

Enjoy your delicious homemade brownies!

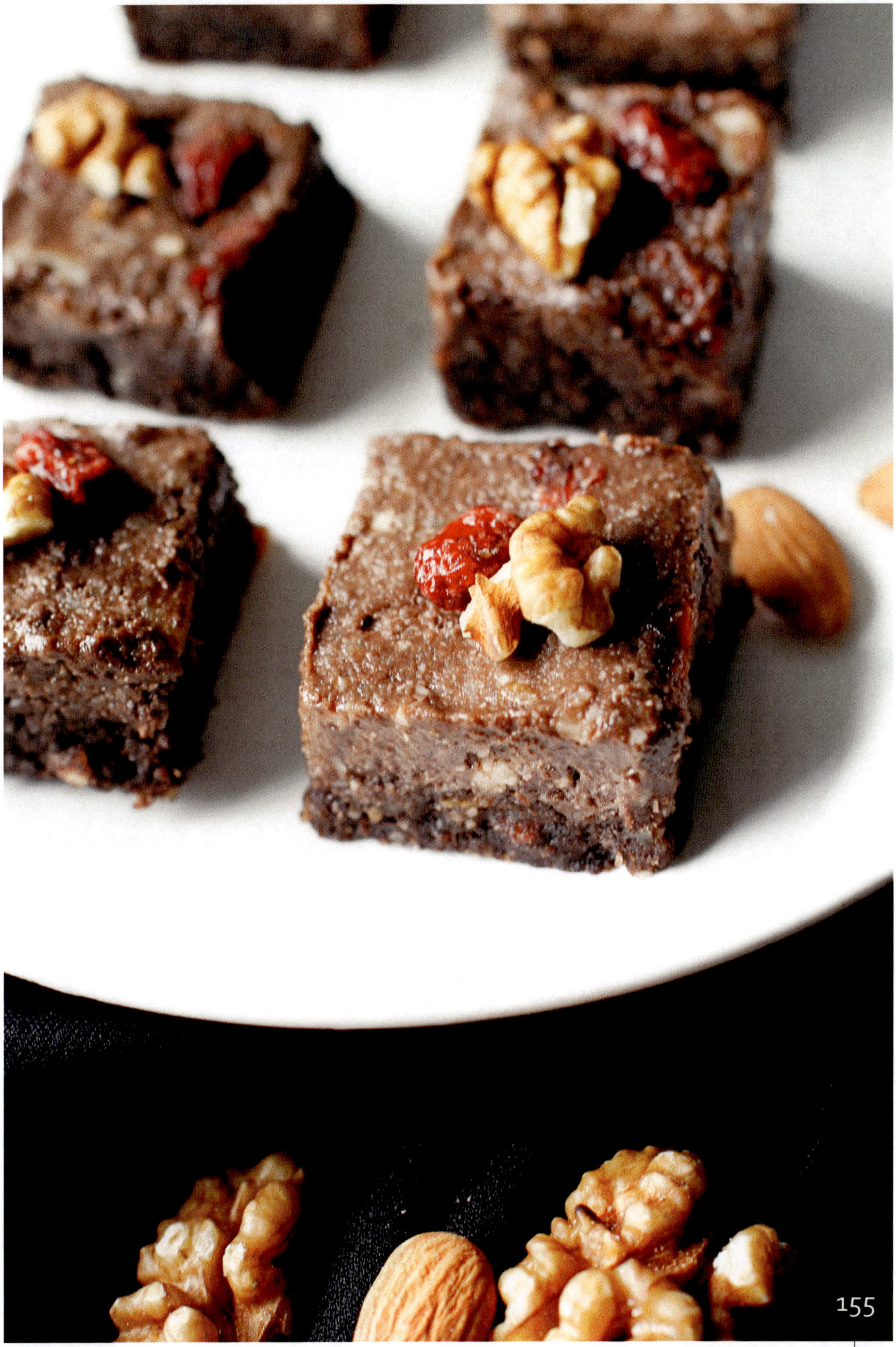

COCONUT ICE CREAM

Lesson 69

Ingredients: 3-4 servings

150g young coconut meat

2 cups water

1 cup macadamia nuts, soaked overnight

15 dates

Zest of 1 lemon

2 tablespoons lemon juice

1/2 teaspoon salt

1 teaspoon vanilla extract

1/4 cup raisins

Instructions

- Place a container in the freezer.
- Blend all ingredients, except raisins, until smooth.
- Pour the mixture into the ice cream container, add raisins, and mix well.
- Freeze for 4-6 hours before serving.
- Enjoy your creamy coconut ice cream!

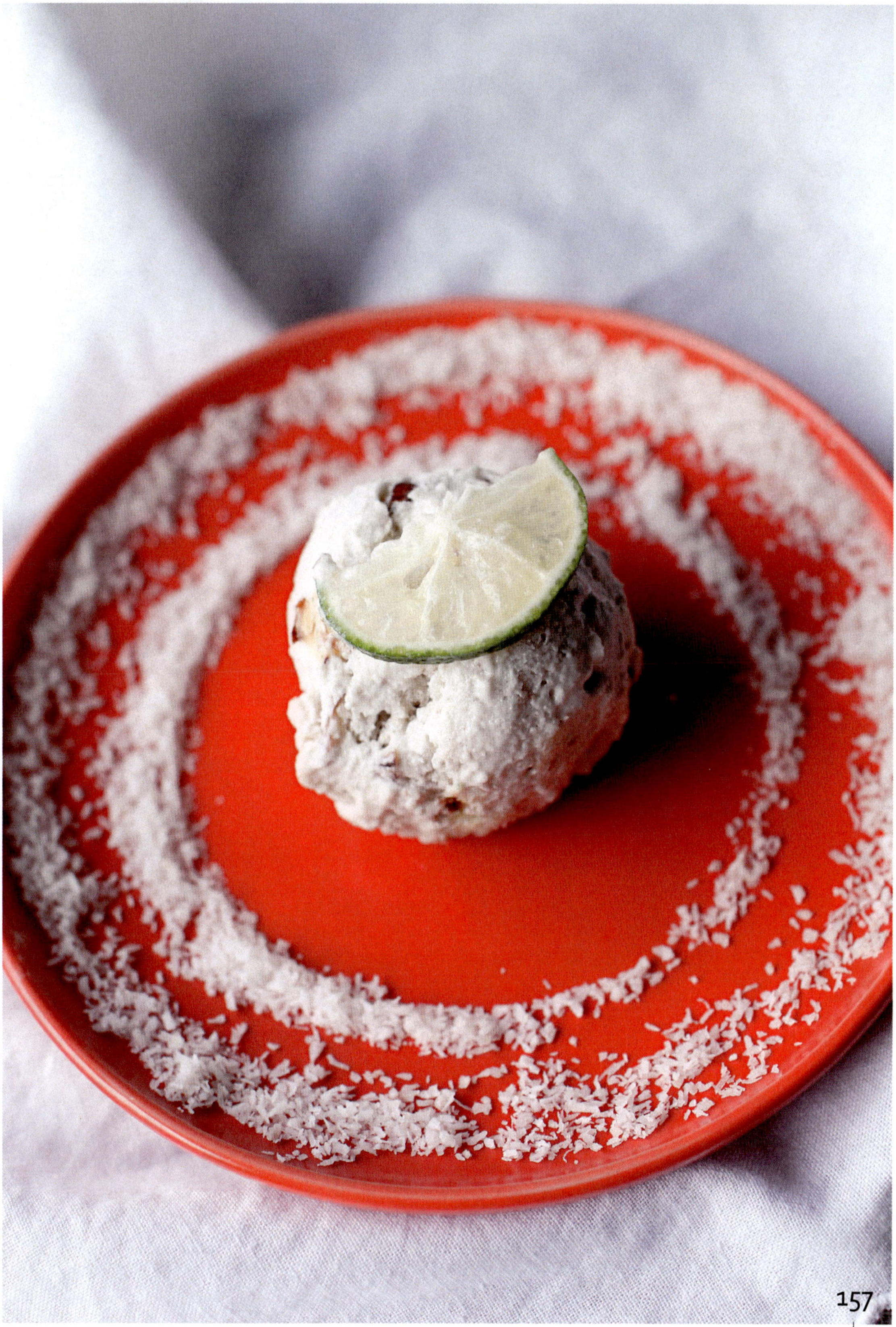

Lesson 70: CHOCOLATE RAISIN ICECREAM

Ingredients: 3-4 servings

2 bananas (approximately 80-100g per banana), peeled and frozen

1/2 cup filtered water

1/2 cup cashews, soaked then drained

5 dates

1/2 teaspoon vanilla extract

1 teaspoon cacao powder

1/2 cup chopped almonds

Instructions

- Place the ice cream container in the freezer.
- In a blender, combine all the ingredients except for the chopped almonds. Blend until smooth.
- After blending, mix in the chopped almonds.
- Pour the mixture into the prepared container and freeze for 4-6 hours before enjoying.
- Indulge in your delicious chocolate raisin ice cream!

159

Table of content

PART 1: INTRODUCTION
Lesson 1: Author introduction 4
Lesson 2: Why raw vegan 6
Lesson 3: Equipment preparation 8
Lesson 4: Tool preparation 12
Lesson 5: Food preparation 14

PART 2: PRINCIPLE OF COOKING
Lesson 6: Sweet flavor 24
Lesson 7: Sour flavor 26
Lesson 8: Salty flavor 28
Lesson 9: Bitter flavor 30
Lesson 10: Umami flavor 33
Lesson 11: Fat 34
Lesson 12: Binding agents 36

PART 3: FOOD HANDLING AND PRESERVATION
Lesson 13: Fruits 40
Lesson 14: Vegetables 43
Lesson 15: Nut and seeds 45

PART 4: KNIFE SKILLS
Lesson 16: Type of knives 48
Lesson 17: Choosing and maintaining knives 49
Lesson 18: Choosing cutting board 50
Lesson 19: Knife grip and cutting technique 51

COOKING RECIPE 52
MENU 53

PART 5: FERMENTED FOOD PRODUCTION
Lesson 20: Vegan yogurt 56
Lesson 21: Vegan cheese 57
Lesson 22: Nutrition-rich kimchi 60
Lesson 23: Pickled vegetables with enriched probiotics 62

PART 6: BASIC RECIPES
Lesson 24: Raw coconut milk 66
Lesson 25: Raw nut butter 67
Lesson 26: Raw plant-based milk 70
Lesson 27: Ketchup 73

PART 7: DEHYDRATION TECHNIQUES
Lesson 28: Apple muffin 76
Lesson 29: Carrot walnut cookies 78
Lesson 30: Banana coconut chia seed pancakes 80
Lesson 31: "Omelette" 82
Lesson 32: Zero waste patties 84
Lesson 33: Fish "cake" 86
Lesson 34: Burger 88
Lesson 35: Kale/perilla snack 89

Lesson 36: Chewy - dried fruit 90

PART 8: DETOX JUICE
Lesson 37: Golden sunshine juice 94
Lesson 38: Detox juice 95
Lesson 39: Violet guardian juice 96
Lesson 40: Red energy juice 97
Lesson 41: Anti-inflammatory juice 98
Lesson 42: Skin-enhancing juice 99

PART 9: SMOOTHIES
Lesson 43: Mango lemon smoothies 102
Lesson 44: Chocolate banana smoothies 103
Lesson 45: Dragon fruit and beetroot smoothies 104

PART 10: TECHNIQUES FOR PROCESSING ROLL DISH
Lesson 46: Sushi maki 108
Lesson 47: Apple tortilla 110
Lesson 48: Kohlrabi dumpling 112
Lesson 49: Beetroot ravioli 114

PART 11: TECHNIQUES FOR MAKING RAW NOODLES
Lesson 50: "Zucchini" with pesto sauce 118
Lesson 51: Pad Thai 120
Lesson 52: Vietnamesese "bun" 122
Lesson 53: Mac n cheese 124

PART 12: PORRIDGE AND SOUP PROCESSING TECHNIQUES
Lesson 54: Carrot soup 126
Lesson 55: Tomato soup 128
Lesson 56: Pumpkin curry soup 130
Lesson 57: Avocado porridge 132

PART 13: SALAD PROCESSING TECHNIQUES
Lesson 58: Russian salad 135
Lesson 59: Mint apricot orange salad 136
Lesson 60: Mixed spinach salad with coconut avocado dressing 138
Lesson 61: Kale salad with cashew 140
Lesson 62: Green papaya salad with tamarind sauce 142
Lesson 63: Banana flower salad 144
Lesson 64: Pomelo salad 146

PART 14: PASTRY AND DESSERT MAKING TECHNIQUES
Lesson 65: Truffle protein 148
Lesson 66: Fruit cheesecake 150
Lesson 67: Mango mousse 152
Lesson 68: Brownies 154
Lesson 69: Coconut icecream 156
Lesson 70: Chocolate rasin icecream 158

Thank you!

Made in United States
Orlando, FL
06 March 2025